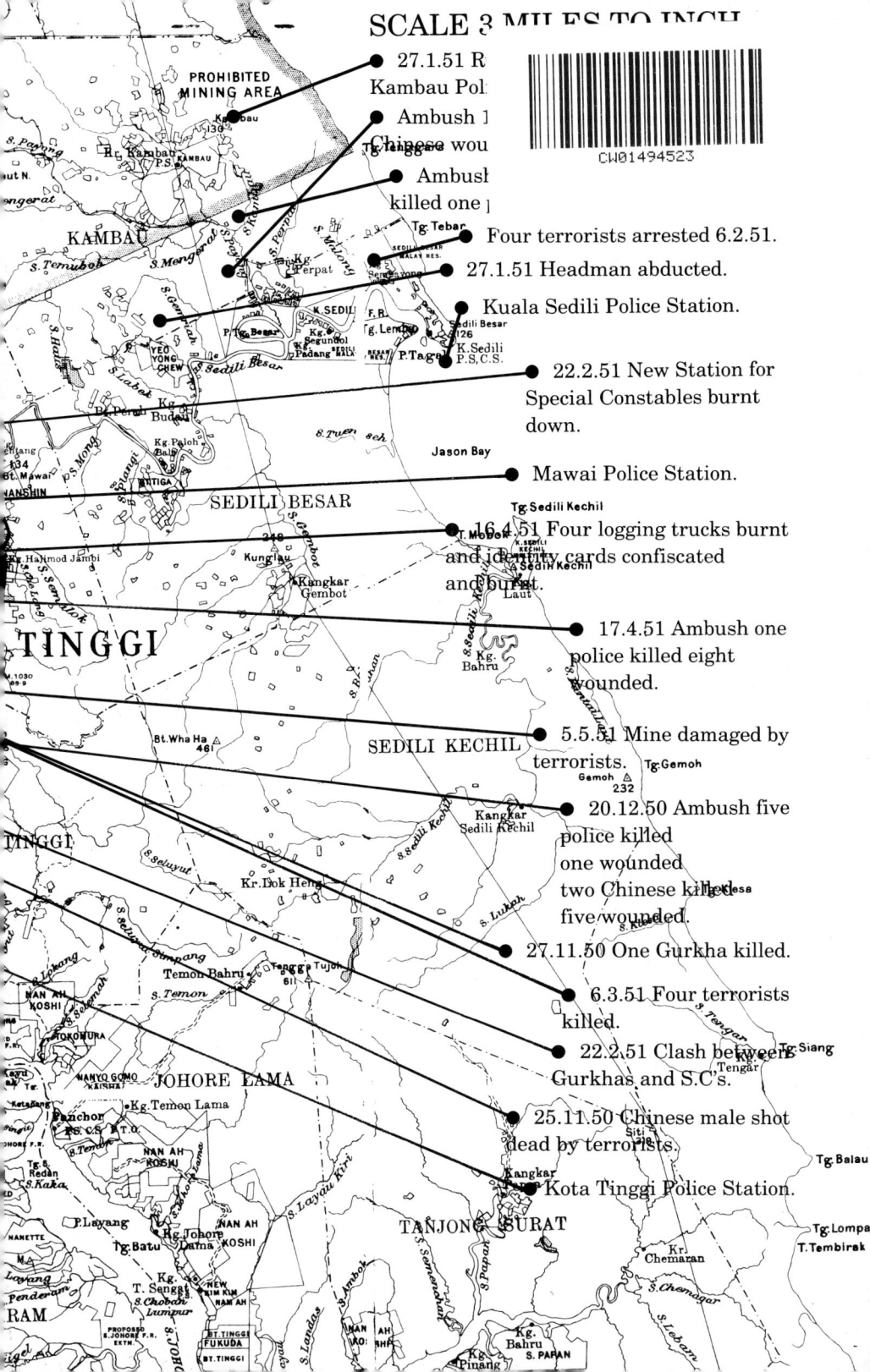

SCALE 3 MILES TO INCH

27.1.51 R...
Kambau Pol...
Ambush 1...
Chinese wou...

Ambush...
killed one...

Four terrorists arrested 6.2.51.

27.1.51 Headman abducted.

Kuala Sedili Police Station.

22.2.51 New Station for Special Constables burnt down.

Mawai Police Station.

16.4.51 Four logging trucks burnt and identity cards confiscated and burnt.

17.4.51 Ambush one police killed eight wounded.

5.5.51 Mine damaged by terrorists.

20.12.50 Ambush five police killed one wounded two Chinese killed five wounded.

27.11.50 One Gurkha killed.

6.3.51 Four terrorists killed.

22.2.51 Clash between Gurkhas and S.C's.

25.11.50 Chinese male shot dead by terrorists.

Kota Tinggi Police Station.

A CHEQUERED CAREER

JOHN MATHIESON
7 DUMBRECK PATH
GLASGOW

G41 5NL

A Chequered Career

W. P. Mathieson

JANUS PUBLISHING COMPANY
London, England

First published in Great Britain 1994
by Janus Publishing Company
Duke House, 37 Duke Street
London W1M 5DF

Copyright © W. P. Mathieson 1994

British Library Cataloguing-in-Publication Data
A catalogue record for this book is available
from the British Library

ISBN 1 85756 135 X

Printed and bound in England by
BPC Wheatons Ltd, Exeter

Contents

Contents

Preface

I decided to write this book because I had the privilege of serving the Crown in Malaya and Tanganyika just before these two countries became independent. The days when British soldiers and policemen patrolled far-flung outposts of the British Empire have vanished and I wanted to record not only the way of life encountered in some of these countries but also the gallantry of the men with whom I served.

I would like this book to serve as a memorial to the 1377 men – officers, rank and file – of the 23rd Indian Division who were killed, wounded or missing in Java, Indonesia during 1945–46. It was also written in memory of the 9093 casualties among the police, military and civilians during the Malayan Emergency from 1948 to 1960, some of whom were colleagues of mine.

Finally, I would like to think it may give hope to some of those facing redundancy, as I did in 1962. I did not give up, but decided to start my own business, and when that failed I started at the bottom of the ladder again and made another career for myself.

I

Early Childhood and School Days

I was number eight of a family of eleven – born on the 18th June 1925 at Roeberry Cottage, South Ronaldsay in the Orkney Isles. My father was foreman at the farm of Kirkhouse of Widewall – one of the largest farms on the island with over 300 acres. His wages were £24 for 6 months, in addition to which he received free milk, 140 lb of oatmeal and $1\frac{1}{2}$ tons of coal. His salary was paid at the end of May and November. Farmworkers at that time were taken on for 6 months at what was known as the feeing market. At the end of this period all were paid off and were free to take up employment with another farmer – or, if they were still wanted by the present employer, or were so inclined, they could be re-employed for a further 6 months.

The basic food in those days consisted of porridge, salt herring or salt fish and potatoes, stewed rabbit and occasionally a piece of pork and cabbage or possibly bully beef. Fresh butchers' meat was generally beyond the means of the average worker.

My father would leave for work at 6 a.m. and return home at 6 p.m. This he did for 6 days a week, and he had to work every alternate Sunday. The farm of Kirkhouse was 2 miles from Roeberry Cottage and this he walked every day. As there was no such thing as child allowance or social security, my mother found it extremely difficult to make ends meet. This

1

meant that one rarely received new clothing – it was a question of wearing clothes handed down from older brothers or sisters.

My schooling started on 26th August 1930. I well remember that day. My elder brother, David, was in charge of me and the distance to the school was $1^1/_2$ miles. He set off ahead and I had to follow. I was wearing a new pair of boots and, not being used to them, I kept tripping on the rough road. I was not very popular. The thing that struck me when plodding along the road was that a new world was opening up before me. Prior to going to school I had never, to my knowledge, left the confines of our large garden area – about an acre of land. In the 1930s there were no school meals and no central heating throughout the school classrooms. Our midday snack, carried from home, usually consisted of bread and jam and a small bottle of milk. During the winter period the teacher in the primary section of the school boiled up a large pot of cocoa. There was no sugar or milk in the cocoa. I had been at school for about a year when a windfall came our way following the loss of the Danish cargo ship *MV Pennsylvania* which ran aground in dense fog on the island of Swona on 27th July 1931. There was no loss of life. The windfall was in the form of crates of herrings in tomato sauce which my father salved from the wreck.

In the autumn of 1931 our family moved to the village of St Margarets Hope, and I exchanged my $1^1/_2$ mile trek, for a 5-minute walk to the local school. Discipline in the school was strict. We had excellent teachers who were highly respected. When coming to or leaving school, if you were wearing a cap and you met the headmaster or deputy headmaster you had to salute them. On the other hand if you met a lady teacher you had to doff your cap. Even in those days of strict discipline there were odd cases of vandalism. One beautiful Saturday morning a gang of schoolboys – I was one of them – left the village and travelled over two hills to an isolated cottage by the shore; it was unoccupied at the time. The younger ones (I was in that category) were being led by two older boys. The

2

cottage was owned by James Sutherland, a Boer War veteran. When we arrived at the house someone started throwing stones at the windows and before we left every pane of glass had been smashed. On the following Monday morning the local policeman, Constable Robert Tulloch, called at the school and it was not long before he had the names of all concerned. One at a time, the culprits were called out of the classrooms and questioned in the ablutions.

The outcome was that the policeman went to a local joiner, James Wards, to get an estimate to replace the glass – £7.0s 0d – a lot of money then. He then went to the fathers of the two older boys and asked if they were prepared to pay £3:10s.0d each to make good the damage; if so there would be no prosecution. This they agreed to do, following which we all got thrashings from our parents. It was fortunate that the fathers of the two older boys were reasonably well off.

Ships that did not pass

Another windfall came our way on the 19th August 1935 when the 3229-ton *MV Gunnaren* struck the island of Swona in dense fog. She was on passage from New York to Gothenburg in Sweden. The crew of 35 were all rescued by the Longhope lifeboat. The cargo included motor cars, radio sets, flour and fruit.

Two years later a third Scandinavian ship was wrecked on the island of Swona, and this time there was loss of life. The ship, the Finnish *MV Johanna Thorden*, struck the island at 5.45 a.m. on the 12th January 1937. The radio operator attempted to send out SOS messages but it was discovered that when the vessel was driven on to the rocks during the gale and high seas the ship struck with such force that the aerial was snapped off and disappeared. Rockets and flares were then sent off to no avail. Twenty minutes after the ship had struck the rocks the lights went out and the only illumination was from two lighthouses, possibly Swona and Stroma. Realising that his ship was doomed, the captain ordered that one of the four lifeboats be launched. Into this lifeboat went two women, two boys and 21 crew members – 25 people in all. Some 20 minutes later the second lifeboat was launched with the remaining 13 crew members, including the captain. The first lifeboat came ashore at Deerness on the mainland of Orkney with three bodies on board, the other 22 people on board had perished in the sea. The second lifeboat, as it approached the shore at Kirkhouse, eastside of South Ronaldsay, capsized in the heavy seas and only eight of the thirteen survived. Thus, out of a total complement of 38 crew and passengers, 30 were lost on that tragic morning. The *Johanna Thorden* had been on her maiden voyage, and had been carrying general cargo. Later she broke up and sacks of flour, cases of apples and oranges, tobacco leaf and chewing gum came ashore.

When I look at the village of St Margarets Hope today I can see that it has changed for the worse over the past 50 years. When I was a boy in the village there were four general merchants, four grocers' shops, three bakers, three clothiers, two footwear shops, two butchers' shops, a jeweller's shop, a cycle shop, a sweet shop, two joinery businesses, two hotels and a post office. Today we have two general merchants, one clothing and footwear shop, two hotels and a post office. The run down was caused mainly by the construction of the Churchill Causeways during World War II which joined the islands of South Ronaldsay, Burray, Glimpsholm and Lambholm to the mainland of Orkney.

An impossible dream

At school, competition in the classrooms was fierce. There was keen competition for the merit prizes which were awarded at the end of every year. During my last year at school, in the advanced division of the St Margarets Hope Higher Grade Public School, the headmaster, on a particular day, invited the three classes in the advanced division to compete for a book on the Prince of Wales Island, Penang, Malaya. The task was to answer 20 questions on geography. Alex Sutherland, the local doctor's daughter, and I tied with 19 correct out of 20. As Alex was in a higher class than I, the headmaster, George Donaldson, awarded the book to me. When handing it over he expressed the hope that one day I would be able to visit this beautiful island. This was the furthest thing from my mind – in fact in those days it seemed an utter impossibility. However, the war changed all this and as you will find out later the impossible turned out to be possible. In June 1939 I sat what was then known as the Day School Certificate (Lower). I gained passes in English, History, Geography, Arithmetic, Algebra, Geometry, Latin, Science and Drawing. Following the examination I was offered two bursaries, each valued at £25, to go on for further education. This was insufficient to pay for accommodation to attend the Grammar School in Kirkwall and to cover incidental expenses. My schooling therefore ended on the 30th June 1939 when I was 14 years and 12 days old.

II

Out to Work

During the month of July I continued to work as a message boy/storeman with R. Rosie & Son, General Merchants, St Margarets Hope, at a salary of 5 shillings (25p) a week. I had carried out weekend and holiday work at the shop for a number of years and I thoroughly enjoyed it. In August I was hired as a harvest hand at the farm of Smiddybanks, St Margarets Hope, doubling my salary to 10 shillings (50p) a week. I was at Smiddybanks on Sunday morning, 3rd September 1939 when war was declared. My life, like those of millions of others, was to be changed. Towards the end of September harvest work was over and I went to the Lyness Naval Base on the island of Hoy where I was employed as a cleaner with a firm of contractors, Baldry Yerburgh and Hutchison. My job was to make up 96 beds (double-deckers), sweep out the huts, clean out, and carry in coal for, the various fires and clean the ablutions. This was a six-day week for which I was paid £0.19s.2d (96p) plus free food and accommodation.

Enemy attacks
I had only been at Lyness for about 2 weeks when, on the night of 14th October 1939, the German U-Boat U-47 entered Scapa Flow through Kirk Sound on the eastern approaches to Scapa Flow and torpedoed the battleship *Royal Oak*. The battleship went down within 25 minutes with the loss of over

800 lives. As a result of this action commercial and local boats were not permitted to traverse Scapa Flow for a considerable time. Destroyers were systematically criss-crossing the Flow searching for more submarines. This meant that although I was only 1 hour's journey from home I did not get home for 7 weeks, and then only through the good offices of Sandy Annal, a local South Ronaldsay man. Sandy had a yawl (small fishing boat) at Longhope and he offered to take the local South Ronaldsay men home for a weekend. We kept outside Scapa Flow, travelling from Longhope, the main village on the island of Hoy, then between the islands of Flotta and Switha, and landed at Quindry, South Ronaldsay.

During my time at Lyness there were numerous air-raid alarms and a number of air raids. When the siren sounded, the instructions were that everyone working in and around the camp area above the Lyness Naval Base had to embark in construction lorries which ferried all the workers up a hill to tunnels which were being constructed for the storage of oil.

On the 17th October 1939 I was travelling near the centre of a convoy of vehicles heading for the tunnels when a German bomber came diving out of the sun, and I clearly saw two bombs falling from the aircraft. After the raid I heard that one of the bombs had struck the battleship *Iron Duke*, and that one of the aircraft involved in the raid had been shot down at Pegal Burn, Hoy. The pilot had bailed out and was captured but the airgunner was killed. This was the first enemy aircraft to be shot down on land in the United Kingdom. Numerous people from the camps trekked miles to get a piece of the aircraft as a souvenir. When getting my own souvenir I saw pieces of flesh scattered on both sides of the burn. I thought at the time that it was rather foolish to transport hundreds of workers along this exposed road to the tunnels. Fortunately the vehicle convoy was never attacked. The German bomber crews were obviously after bigger and better targets.

After the sinking of the battleship *Royal Oak*, Winston

Churchill, then First Lord to the Admiralty, flew up to Orkney and decided to block off the four entrances on the east side of Scapa Flow with solid barriers. In April 1940, with the construction of the tunnels and tank storage areas in the Hoy hills almost completed, I went to the island of Hunda where Balfour Beatty & Co were constructing a barrier between the islands of Hunda and Burray. Why this construction was undertaken I do not know, as it did nothing for the defence of Scapa Flow. It is possible that the military intended to install anti-aircraft guns on the island of Hunda but nothing ever materialised. On the other hand it may have been a practice run before tackling the bigger barriers.

I was still only 14 years old and was now employed as a cleaner in a small camp on Hunda. Hunda was provisioned with food and all other necessities of life by David Wylie, a popular and well-known seaman from the Burray village. David was always up to tricks. One day we had an extremely low tide and with such low tides it was possible to catch lobsters below certain rocks. David was down on the beach with the camp boss Bennett and myself. He came across two rocks each having a small cave-like entrance at its base. Twice he pushed in a thin piece of reinforcing rod; on both occasions lobsters grabbed the iron rod and Davie gently pulled the lobsters out. Bennett was very taken by this and asked Davie if he could have a go. We came upon another likely rock and Davie handed over the iron rod to Bennett before moving quickly around to the other side of the rock. When Davie saw the end of the iron rod appearing he jammed it with a stick. Bennett shouted that he had got something. 'Pull it out, gently,' said Davie.

'He must be a big bugger because I can't move it,' came the reply. Needless to say Bennett soon found out why he couldn't move it.

Rations at the time were pretty meagre so during the early summer of 1940 I was sent around the island to collect gulls' eggs, resulting in some good fries and omelettes.

When the Hunda barrier was completed in late 1940/ early 1941 I was moved by Balfour Beatty & Co to St Margarets Hope pier where a naval camp and mine shed were under construction. I was employed as a mess boy in a small canteen at the farm of Smiddybanks near the pier. When this was completed I was moved to the Ward Hill in South Ronaldsay where one of the early radar stations was under construction. I was still not yet 16 years old. Initially at the Ward Hill I was employed as a 'nipper', doing all the odd jobs such as brewing up tea for the construction workers, which meant walking half a mile to get water or cycling to the village of St Margarets Hope 5 miles away for anything required by the workers. Later I was employed as an assistant to Tom Thomson, a local joiner employed by Balfour Beatty & Co on maintenance work at the large naval camp on the Ward Hill.

In early 1942 I was moved to the Burray barrier where I was delighted to find myself again in the company of David Wylie, based at the Burray pier. My job was to work with Admiralty engineers sounding the depths between the islands of Burray and South Ronaldsay. Following the dumping of rock by the Blondin machine, about which I shall say more later, I had to manoeuvre a dinghy from one end of the barrier to the other and to hold the dinghy in position whilst the two engineers seated at the stern of the dinghy took soundings at 6-ft intervals. This was quite a difficult operation as the tides between Burray and South Ronaldsay (a strip of water known as Water Sound) raced through at a speed of 8 to 10 knots, except during the slack-water period. The dumping of loose rock proved unsuccessful. The rock would appear above the surface almost all the way across while after an easterly or westerly gale no sign of rock could be seen. It was then decided that the 5 tons of rock would be placed in wire bolsters, the open end being secured with a spiral wire. This proved to be the answer. The South Ronaldsay end of the barrier, which was much the shallower of the two ends, was subcontracted to W. Tawse & Son. They dumped rock in their section by means of a locomotive on rails with side-tipping skips. The Blondin machine masts on the islands of Burray and South Ronaldsay were 180 feet high and to lay a pattern of bolsters the masts were moved from the upright position to 25 ft either side. To do this a gang of six men operated hand winches – three easing off 25 ft of cable and the other three winding in 25 ft of cable. The six operators then climbed into the box which dumped the rocks and were transported to the other island where they carried out the same operation (25 feet either side from the upright position was the maximum distance the masts were allowed to go). A row of bolsters was then dumped and after this the masts were taken in 5 ft to 20 ft from the upright position, then to 15 ft, 10 ft, 5 ft and back to the upright position. In Holm Sound during one of these operations the box carrying the six operators struck the sea halfway across and the operators were catapulted into the sea. Two of them were drowned. Following this accident the mast crew working on the Burray/South Ronaldsay barrier had to sit on the steel arm which picked up the box and were ferried across in that fashion. All one had to hold on to were chains which went up to the pulley which ran along the main cable.

One day, after altering the mast on the South Ronaldsay side, we travelled back along the cable to Burray. We were about 160 feet above the ground. It was not possible to travel on the Blondin machine at low level without the box because the steel lifting arm would twist around and as a result all cables would become entangled. We were waiting to be lowered at the Burray terminus but nothing happened and it started to drizzle heavily. Someone shouted that the lowering cable had come off the pulley at the top of the mast and that we would have to hang on until they had the matter rectified. It took half an hour and we eventually hit hard ground. There was no such thing as Health and Safety at work in those days.

When not working with the Admiralty engineers I was attached to David Wylie at the Burray pier. David was in charge of a gang of Italian prisoners of war who unloaded the various cargo ships that called. The Italians were a very friendly crowd and I got on well with the crane driver, Aleroni Guilio. He spoke very good English. One day, when lifting a locomotive off a ship, the crane toppled over but Aleroni fortunately jumped clear and was not injured. The Italians were incredibly good at making things out of old pieces of metal or wood. They made rings to measure, cigarette lighters and beautiful model cars. Some of the cars had sliding roofs and were in fact cigarette boxes.

With the dropping of rock in bolsters the barrier began to take shape and there was then no longer any need to work with the Admiralty engineers. I was then sent as flagman on the barrier to instruct the operator of the Blondin machine where to stop the box of rocks and when to tip the box. This was a case of filling in gaps.

Home Guard

On reaching the age of 17 I joined the local Home Guard. Training took place at the Hillside army camp in South Ronaldsay. There were two platoons of Home Guard in South Ronaldsay, one stationed at the Hillside Camp and the other at an army camp in the south of the island. A permanent staff instructor with the rank of company sergeant major was attached to us. We were initially issued with the Canadian Ross rifle .300 calibre and later with the Lee Enfield .303. Other weapons allocated included the Sten gun, Spiget mortar and Smith gun (a 3-inched smooth-barrelled piece of artillery). We did fire the Spiget mortar – an amazing piece of weaponry issued only, I believe, to the Home Guard. I never fired the Smith gun and don't think it would have been advisable except in a dire emergency.

We had a very keen platoon with practically no absentees at training sessions. Some of our members were of World War I vintage and great characters. On one occasion we were mobilised when there was a fear of midget submarine landings. We were all issued with firearms which we took to our homes

11

so that we would not be caught out in the event of a callout. This however did not materialise. During my 2 years and 3 months in the Home Guard I moved from the rank of private to colour sergeant. When I reached the age of 19 (1943) I was moved under the Direction of Manpower Regulations from Balfour Beatty & Co to the Rinibar Quarry, Hoxa, South Ronaldsay. I was then employed by Glasgow contractors H.M. Murray & Co who were mainly concerned with the upkeep of roads for the military and the opening up of new roads.

III

Military Service

On the 14th September 1944 I was called up to serve in His Majesty's Armed Forces. I was notified that as I was a member of the Home Guard I had to travel in uniform but had to remove the shoulder flash on my tunic (Orkney No. 2 battalion, Home Guard). With this removed I looked like a full colour sergeant in the Seaforth Highlanders. The Home Guard in Orkney wore the Scottish regiments' balmoral plus the Seaforth Highlanders' badge fixed over a square of MacKenzie tartan – the tartan worn by the Seaforths. This proved advantageous at first but embarrassing later. On arriving at Scrabster from Stromness in the Orkneys I was met by a jeep from the sergeants' transit mess at Thurso and taken to the sergeants' mess for lunch. Following lunch I was transported to Thurso railway station on my way to the 11th Infantry Training Centre (Seaforth & Cameron), Pinefield Camp, Elgin, Morayshire. On arrival at Elgin railway station, some other conscripts and I were marshalled by a lance corporal and taken in a 3-ton truck to Pinefield Camp. On arriving in our allocated barrack block a lance corporal approached me with a razor blade and said, 'Get them off'. He was referring to the three stripes and crown, the insignia of a colour sergeant/staff sergeant. I had no option but to comply. Following this the lance corporal asked if any of the new recruits could play musical instruments. About seven hands went up and after he had recorded their names and what type of instrument they played he ordered them to report to the cookhouse at 6 p.m. for spud bashing.

It never paid to volunteer for anything in the army. The initial training at Pinefield Camp consisted of 6 weeks' basic training following which recruits were asked which branch of the service they wished to serve in e.g., infantry, signals, royal electrical mechanical engineers, royal army service corps, royal engineers, pioneers, etc. There was of course no guarantee that you got into the unit/branch of your choice. I volunteered for the Seaforth Highlanders and when asked why, I said that I already had two brothers in the Seaforths and why not make it three. If you were fit you were never turned down for the infantry. My elder brother, David, a corporal in the 2nd battalion Seaforth Highlanders, 51st Highland Division, had been taken prisoner at St Valery in France at the time of the Dunkirk evacuation. He was at that time in Stalag 20B prisoner of war camp in Poland. My other brother, Peter, also a corporal, was in the 5th battalion Seaforth Highlanders (Duke of Sutherlands' Own). They wore a different tartan and cap badge from other battalions of the Seaforths. He had served in the re-formed 51st Highland Division in the North African campaign and had been wounded at El Alamein and Wadi Akarit in North Africa; he'd been wounded a third time at Franca Fonte in Sicily. He was eventually 'graded down' and sent to a home posting. He was at that time stationed at Redford Barracks, Edinburgh, but during my infantry training at Pinefield Camp he was posted to the camp in the administration field.

This now entailed 10 weeks' infantry training and, apart from being chased from pillar to post from early morning to late at night, nothing particularly exciting happened. Following the training I was posted to the 9th battalion Seaforth Highlanders at Hoddam Castle, near Annan, Dumfriesshire for 5 weeks' battalion training. When we arrived at the guard room at the main gate to Hoddam Castle our accommodation was allocated and we were told to be sure to read the daily orders. I did this after getting settled in and found that my name was down for quarter guard in two days' time and that at 2 p.m. the next day I had to report to the guard room with three others to be drilled in quarter guard mounting by the regimental sergeant major (RSM).

The quarter guard was and is the bullshit guard at all infantry depots and can be fairly complicated to newcomers. RSM Atkinson put us through our paces for over an hour and his last orders were that we were all to report to the regimental barber for a haircut. This order I duly complied with, to be told by the barber that I did not need a trim. At 9.30 a.m. on the following morning the complete guard – a sergeant, lance corporal and four private soldiers – was thoroughly inspected by the RSM prior to the arrival of the duty officer of the day who carried out the official mounting of the guard at 10 a.m. This was in the middle of winter, and the dress comprised battledress, boots and gaiters, overcoat, steel helmet, belt and bayonet, small pack and rifle. When the RSM was inspecting the rear of the guard he hit my pack with his cane and shouted, 'Take a step forward, man.'

With this order I complied.

He then said, 'Am I hurting you?'

'No sir,' I replied.

'Take another step forward, man,' he shouted . . .

'Am I hurting you now?'

'No sir.'

'I bloody well ought to be, I am standing on your hair.'

He then ordered the sergeant of the guard to put me on a charge for not getting my hair cut.

After the ceremony of the mounting of the guard we took over from the quarter guard going off duty. Of the four privates on the guard the smartest and best dressed was selected as stick man for the next 24 hours. He carried out his duties as an orderly at the commanding officer's office. The remaining three carried out duties at the guard room.

One was posted outside the guard room and marched 15 paces back and forth in front of the guard room for 2 hours. You could intermittently stand at ease. All officers had to be saluted. Officers up to the rank of captain received a 'butt' salute, majors a 'present arms' and officers of higher rank – the entire guard was turned out for them – also received the 'present arms'. One day, when on quarter guard, I saw the RSM about 100 yards away and a private soldier coming towards him. As the RSM wore an officers' pattern balmoral and kilt the poor unfortunate soldier thought the RSM was an officer and started saluting him at least 20 yards before they were due to meet. I heard a scream from the RSM and saw the soldier running towards him. The outcome was that the soldier was given 7 days' confined to barracks for saluting the RSM, he not holding the King's Commission.

In my case the sergeant of the guard, a Black Watch sergeant, who had just returned from the fighting on the northern sector of the western front with the 51st Highland Division, said that he had no intention of following the RSM's orders by putting me on a charge; he added that if he had had the RSM in France and Germany all the bullshit would have been knocked out of him. The 5 weeks' battalion training at Hoddam Castle and all over the Dumfriesshire hills passed off without incident.

As the war in Europe was drawing to a close there did not appear to be a great demand for reinforcements for the battalions in Europe and one was held in suspense. During the waiting period I was sent on two courses – the first to Morpeth in Northumberland for a week to learn how to construct dry latrines. The second was a 6-week course at Shoeburyness near Southend in Essex. This was a course on the stripping, assembling, firing and general maintenance of the six pounder anti-tank gun. One was also taught how to drive the tracked Lloyd carrier – the vehicle used for towing the anti-tank gun.

Tragedy on V-E day

I was still with the 9th battalion at Hoddam Castle on V-E Day, 8th May 1945. On that day I was with a company of Seaforths on the Dumfriesshire hills. We were firing the 2 inch mortar. There were two men to a mortar and we were stretched out in a line along the hillside. The object of the exercise was that the first mortar team fired smoke and the team next to them fired high explosive at the smoke target thus created. During this exercise something went wrong. A team on one of the mortars firing high explosive turned the firing knob, and there was an immediate explosion which blew the mortar to pieces and killed the soldiers instantly.

India

At the end of May 1945 I got posted to the 1st battalion Seaforth Highlanders in India. On 7th June 1945 I embarked on *MV Sobeiski*, a Polish troopship at Greenock, and headed for Bombay. The journey took 23 days and was quite pleasant and uneventful. We travelled via Gibraltar through the Mediterranean, Suez Canal, Red Sea and on to Bombay. In the Suez Canal we met a troopship heading for the UK and there was much banter from the other side – 'Get your knees brown! Get some service in!' At Port Said I was amazed to see how well the young Egyptian boys could swim and dive. They swam around the troopship and kept shouting for money. Shillings and sixpences were thrown into the water. They would dive after the money and never fail to recover it. Some of the smart types on board wrapped pennies in silver paper. When the young divers found that they had been 'done' there came a torrent of abuse. They knew all the right words.

On 30th June 1945 *MV Sobeiski* docked at Bombay and all troops on board were transported to the Deulali transit camp where one got sorted out. This camp was anything but hygienic. Flies were everywhere and the dry latrines were not up to the standard of those I had been taught to construct at

17

Morpeth a few months earlier. The latrines comprised a deep pit, about 30 ft long and 4 ft wide. A large baton, about a foot from the edge of the latrine, ran along the entire length of the pit. This was the seat on which one squatted, frequently with five to ten other squaddies. There was no privacy apart from a sacking fence which surrounded the latrine.

After a week sampling the Deulali transit camp facilities I was glad to be told that I was off to join the 1st Seaforths at Satpur. On arrival at the Satpur tented camp I was notified that I had to report to No. 8 platoon, C company. When giving my personal particulars to the platoon sergeant, Jimmy Davie, he noted that I came from St Margarets Hope, Orkney.

'Do you know a family in South Ronaldsay called Simison?' he asked.

I told him that there was only one Simison family in South Ronaldsay and that prior to being called up I had worked with Jock, the head of the family, at the Rinibar Quarry, Hoxa, South Ronaldsay.

'I am married to Jock Simison's daughter, Kate,' he said.

Jimmy hailed from Edinburgh and was a plumber by trade. Although I did not know his wife personally I told him that I knew most of the family. A small world.

From 7th July to almost the end of August we underwent extensive training, including route marches, embussing and debussing from vehicles and assault landings. One of the battalion route marches which lasted a week went all wrong for C company. On one of the days of this route march we were following D company. With such route marches the three platoons of the company with their respective platoon headquarters, comprising platoon officer, platoon sergeant, 2 inch mortarmen and runner, together with the staff from company headquarters, were divided up into sections. Each platoon consisted of three 10- or 12-man sections together with platoon headquarters, making a total of about 40 men. When on the move, 10 yards separated one man from another, so the distance between the first soldier and last could be 400 yards.

Sections marched on alternate sides of the road. It was now late in the evening – the time when the battalion normally moved off the road into the jungle, set up night bivouac and posted sentries. For some reason the platoon of D company, which we were gaily following, had fallen behind and had lost the remainder of the battalion. The entire battalion with the exception of D company's platoon and all of C company had moved into the jungle and we were plodding on.

After we had gone about 2 miles beyond the point where we should have entered the jungle a furious commanding officer riding in a jeep caught up with us and told our company commander, Major Campbell-Baldwin, that we had lost the rest of the battalion. It was then we heard that the platoon of D company and all of C company were to be punished for not keeping up with the rest of the battalion. Our company commander remonstrated with the commanding officer, pointing out that it was not our fault. The CO would not listen to him.

Our punishment was that when the exercise was over, the final point being 17 miles from camp, the rest of the battalion would be ferried back in vehicles but we would do a forced march back to camp. Well, we did this – not a soul fell out. No rest breaks were taken and in fact we were moving so fast that the company piper could not play until we marched into camp playing *The Green Hills of Tyrol*. We were paraded before the commanding officer's office and I felt that remorse had set in because all he did was to ask our commanding officer to dismiss us. Major Campbell-Baldwin, an excellent company commander, thanked us for our spirit and determination. Colonel E. H. B. Neill, the commanding officer, marched the 17 miles as well. All our extensive training, including assault landing exercises, was tied up with the forthcoming invasion of Malaya.

Following the dropping of atomic bombs on Hiroshima and Nagasaki on 6th August 1945 and the subsequent order from Emperor Hirohito of Japan to his armed forces on 14th

August to surrender, everything was in turmoil. No one was prepared to embark immediately on troopships and head for Malaya or anywhere else in South East Asia. However, on 30th August 1945 the 1st Seaforths embarked on *MV Bossevain*, a Dutch troopship at Bombay, and, with other troopships carrying the remainder of the 23rd Indian Division, sailed for Malaya. The 1st brigade of the 23rd Indian Division comprised the 1st Battalion Patiala Regiment, 1/16 Punjab Regiment, 1st Seaforths and 178 Field Regiment Royal Artillery. On the morning of 12th September 1945 we arrived off Port Dickson about halfway up the west coast of Malaya. As we were unsure of the state of affairs in Malaya it was decided that a proper assault landing would be made. This entailed climbing down rope nets slung over the side of the troopship and, at platoon strength, embarking into assault landing craft. This was accomplished without loss and we were ashore near Port Dickson at about 5 p.m. After getting sorted out into company formations at 6 p.m. the brigade moved off to its destination, which was Seremban, 25 miles away. We arrived there as dawn was breaking. When passing through Malay villages on the way to Seremban, members of the Malayan People's Anti-Japanese Army were very much in evidence. They had come out of the jungle and had taken over all the villages. They were dressed in jungle-green uniforms with peaked cap and communist red star.

After taking the surrender of the Japanese in and around Seremban and Jasin in the state of Negri Sembilan we were told that we were on the move again, this time to Java in Indonesia.

Indonesia

On 28th September 1945, after a 5-day voyage in landing craft infantry vessels, the 1st Seaforths docked at Tandjoeng Priok Docks, Jakarta. We were followed the same day by the battalions of the Patialas and Punjab Regiments, together with

178 Field Regiment Royal Artillery, which made up the 1st Brigade of the 23rd Indian Division. No. 8 platoon, C company, Seaforth Highlanders, were immediately dispatched to guard the Tjedang Internment Camp, which held 9000 Dutch women and children and 1000 men. My duties – at the time I held the rank of local acting unpaid lance corporal – were to post guards around an area of the perimeter fence and regularly visit these guards. Indonesian extremists frequently fired into the camp area during the hours of darkness.

Our purpose in going to Java was to accept the surrender of the Japanese and arrange the repatriation of prisoners of war and internees; of the latter there were over 100 000. It can be no exaggeration to say that no one who landed at that time had the faintest idea of what was going on. The situation was so confused that it was difficult to imagine what would happen on the following day. What had actually happened was that, on 17th August 1945, 3 days after the surrender of the Japanese, the Indonesians, who wanted freedom from the Dutch, declared their independence. This they were able to do with the support of the Japanese, who had trained a fair-sized Indonesian armed force.

On 7th October I was appointed paid lance corporal, and a few days later I was posted with a section of men to guard a small Eurasian internment camp behind the Hotel Des Indes in the centre of Jakarta. This turned out to be a nice quiet posting in a cul-de-sac but was not to last for long. At the end of October my section was recalled to join No. 8 platoon under Sergeant Davie; the platoon was guarding warehouses near the dock area. This proved to be a much more active area and there was looting and shooting on most nights. We were so thin on the ground that Japanese prisoners of war were issued with a rifle and five rounds of ammunition to assist in guarding the docks. They were supervised by one of their own noncommissioned officers under the supervision of a noncommissioned officer from the regiment.

As is inevitable in insurrections like these, atrocities

21

occurred now and again. The worst one occurred in the village of Bekassi, only 7 miles from Jakarta, after the forced landing of a Dakota aircraft carrying troops. The Dakota, with an RAF crew of four and 18 Indian soldiers – reinforcements for the 2nd Hyderabad Regiment – left Jakarta for Sourabaya on Friday 23rd November 1945. The aircraft was unable to land at Sourabaya due to bad weather and returned to Jakarta. When only 4 miles from Jakarta the pilot had to make a forced landing. The troops and aircrew all escaped uninjured. They were seen from the air standing around the burning aircraft. Indonesian villagers came out to meet them and instead of being led to Jakarta they were taken to the village of Bekassi which had a long-standing reputation for cruelty. It is not known where the soldiers and RAF crew were kept on the Friday night but on the following night, Saturday, they were incarcerated in the Bekassi jail, having been led through the village naked with their hands tied behind them. Next day, Sunday 25th November, at about 2 p.m. the survivors from the plane crash were taken from the jail one at a time, still naked and with their hands tied behind them. They were taken to the edge of a steep bank of the Tjileungsar River and their captors, Indonesian extremists, in the presence of about 50 villagers and with the help of some of them, slashed these men to death with parangs and tumbled them down the bank into a pit. Earth was then shovelled upon the bodies.

On 1st December a strong force of 1/16 Punjab Regiment, supported by tanks and a troop of 25 pounders from 178 Field Regiment Royal Artillery from the 23rd Indian Division, went to Bekassi to search for the bodies of the crew and passengers of the Dakota. A local woman, the wife of an Ambonese soldier, indicated the spot where the men had been murdered; 22 bodies were recovered – 18 Indian soldiers and four British airmen. They were brought back to Jakarta and all were cremated together. The village of Bekassi was deserted. On 26th December 1945, when still stationed at the Tandjoeng Priok docks, I was promoted to the rank of corporal.

In early February 1946 the battalion moved to Bogor, 40 miles from Jakarta, and remained there for only 10 days. Our main task was to carry out screening operations in a bid to rid the town of Indonesian extremists. Bogor had been from 1745 onwards the seat of the Dutch governor general whose magnificent palace is located close to the now world-famous botanical gardens. These gardens were founded in 1817 by Sir Stamford Raffles and house in the region of 15 000 flourishing specimens of the indigenous flora. More than 3000 different orchids and the world's largest flower, 'Rafflesia', may be viewed there. A magnificent avenue ran through the centre of the town with fine old houses standing well back from the road.

The battalion then moved on to Bandoeng, some 120 miles inland from Jakarta, standing on a plateau 2300 feet above sea level in a cool and pleasant climate. Many Dutch government institutions and colleges were established in Bandoeng and it was then referred to as the inland capital of Java. On arrival in Bandoeng to join up with 37 brigade of the 23rd Indian Division we found that the town was divided into two by a railway line. The area south of the railway line was held by Indonesian extremists while we held the other half of the town to the north of the railway line. Road blocks were erected on all main and side roads by both sides and fire was exchanged frequently.

Pause for thought

During a lull one day when I was in charge of a road block with a section of men, an Indonesian officer in uniform carrying a white flag emerged from one of their road blocks and started walking slowly towards our road block. He was met by Jimmy Davie, our platoon sergeant. The Indonesian officer spoke perfect English and the gist of his conversation was that he could not understand why we, the British, after fighting successfully for 6 long years, were here in Indonesia losing men needlessly when we should all be home. The platoon sergeant explained that the only reason we were in Indonesia was to effect the surrender of the Japanese and to get all prisoners of war and internees repatriated. The Indonesian officer pointed out that we were in fact assisting the yellow-bellied Dutch to get back into their country and take it over again. There was a lot of truth in what he said. After handing over propaganda leaflets and being assured of a safe passage to his own lines he shook hands and departed. Half an hour later the Indonesians opened up from their road block.

I was still on duty at this particular road block on the 10th March 1946 when 49 brigade of the 23rd Indian Division decided to secure a part of Bandoeng by capturing Lembang, a garden town a few miles from Bandoeng where the Indonesians had seized all the Dutch market gardens and farms. This operation was a complete success. On the same day, 10th March, a Sunday, a large convoy of vehicles containing food for the military, prisoners of war and internees, plus stores and ammunition passed through Bogor on its way to Bandoeng. The convoy was being escorted by the 1st battalion Patiala Regiment. Also travelling with the convoy was the rearguard party of the Seaforth Highlanders. The convoy was stopped by a road block about 8 miles to the west of Soekaboemi. The convoy commander, the commanding officer of the 1st battalion Patiala Regiment, reported that there appeared to be several hundred extremists between there and Soekaboemi and the extremists seemed prepared to make a fight of it. The convoy proceeded without incident for a time and it looked as if it might get into the harbour area at Soekaboemi without fighting. At about 6.30 p.m., however, the extremists opened fire and a heavy attack developed. It was not until 9.00 p.m. that the last vehicle got into the harbour area.

The fighting continued throughout the night, the extremists using small arms, machine guns and mortars. By morning the convoy escort had suffered eight killed and 25 wounded. A half squadron of Sherman tanks of the 13th Indian Lancers which were in Bogor were asked on the morning of 11th March to join up with the convoy at Soekaboemi. Their progress was very slow; the leading tank struck a mine when about 15 miles west of Soekaboemi and suffered damage to its tracks. As there was no room for other tanks to get past, the road being narrow with a steep slope on the one side and a drop into rice fields on the other, further progress was impossible – so the tank crews and escort party of the 2nd Indian Grenadiers stayed where they were for the night of 11th March. They had already suffered one killed and 20 wounded.

On the morning of Monday 11th March the main convoy pushed on from Soekaboemi but owing to stiff opposition progress was very slow and the convoy harboured that night 8 miles out of Soekaboemi. On the same day a force from the 5th battalion Rajputana Rifles was sent out from Bandoeng to make contact with the main convoy. It met many road blocks and there was some fighting in which two men were killed and 19 wounded.

On Tuesday 12th March the tank column beat off heavy attacks which lasted all morning. A very accurate air drop was made, supplying much-needed ammunition and spare parts. Two companies of the 1st Patiala Regiment were sent back from the main convoy to help with the protection of the tanks. The tanks eventually got started and came to within 4 miles of Soekaboemi before they had to stop for the night. The main convoy remained stationary and troops from the 5th Rajputana Rifles made contact with the main convoy; but later they withdrew to protect an important bridge halfway back to Bandoeng. On the same day, 12th March, a strong column of troops from the 1st brigade comprising 1st Seaforths, 1/16 Punjab Regiment with the 3/10 Gurkha Rifles went out from Bandoeng under the command of Brigadier Wingrove with the task of extricating the convoys.

On Wednesday 13th March the tank convoy joined up with the main convoy of vehicles and they harboured together for the night. The 1st brigade encountered many road blocks and there was some fighting, one man being killed and four wounded. On Thursday an early start was made with the convoy crossing the vital bridge safely – but it met heavy fire from snipers and machine guns at several places further on. Fighting to the end, the convoy reached Andir Airfield on the outskirts of Bandoeng at 7 p.m. Arrangements had been made for the quick dispersal of the vehicles, and the casualties, numbering 103, were quickly in bed in the 23rd Indian General Hospital. The convoy, which had been on the road for 5 days, had had to fight almost every inch of the way from Soekaboemi to Bandoeng. Just before it arrived there the garrison troops in Bandoeng were paraded and asked to donate blood. This was the first occasion on which I gave blood.

In the meantime things were not standing still in Bandoeng. There had been several skirmishes with extremists south of the railway line dividing the town. The night before plans to recapture the southern part of the town were put into operation, extremists sabotaged many buildings and warehouses there. Many explosions were heard and the flames lit up the night sky. Public buildings and Chinese property were the worst sufferers and many Chinese refugees fled over the railway line seeking shelter in the northern part of the town. Troops from the 49th brigade 23rd Indian Division moved into the southern area in the early morning and after making excellent progress the divisional commander decided to occupy the whole of the southern part of the town that day to prevent further destruction of property. By evening, at the cost of a very few casualties, the whole of the southern area had been cleared.

After this operation I was posted with a section of men to Lembang, about 8 miles outside Bandoeng. We were billeted at the Lembang Observatory on the top of a hill with a magnificent view of the surrounding countryside. At this time Dutch troops were gradually taking over and in early April 1946 the 1st Seaforths were posted to the Poentjak Pass with brigade headquarters at Tandjoer. Our duties were then to patrol the mountainous roads through the pass, the scene of many ambushes. On one patrol in April 1946 the entire platoon set off at daybreak on an 8-mile patrol down the road to contact a platoon of D company who were guarding an important bridge. The full platoon comprised 40 men. The first section took the left of the road, 10 yards between every man, followed by platoon headquarters on the right; then came the second section on the left of the road and finally the third section on the right. The first section set up a fast pace which meant that some of my men taking up the rear of the patrol had to run at times to keep up. I got moans about this from my section but told them, 'Don't worry, we will be the leading section on the way back and we will set a brisk pace then.'

On reaching the D company platoon we had a rest and then set off on the return journey. Private Garvie was the leading man in our section and I told him to set a brisk pace. After travelling for about 3 miles I could hear Jimmy Davie, the platoon sergeant away down the road, shouting 'Ease your f . . . . . . step.' We pretended that we did not hear him and carried on. Well, it didn't pay. When we got back to company headquarters Jimmy Davie lined my section up and said that since we had deliberately disobeyed orders to slow down we would have to go back down the road after lunch, contact the platoon of D company again, and then return to base. This meant doing a 32-mile round trip in one day. Nothing for it but to obey orders.

We set off after lunch and arrived at the platoon of D company at about 3.30 p.m. They were surprised to see us again. After explaining to the platoon officer what had happened I asked if it would be possible for him, after we had had a rest, to arrange for my section to be driven 6 miles up the road where we would hide up in the jungle for 2 hours; later, having only 2 miles to go, we would be able to work up a good sweat before marching into the company lines. The platoon officer was all for this and we set off in his 15 cwt truck. We disembarked 2 miles from camp and rested for 2 hours. Then we got on the road again and set up a cracking pace. Word had got around about our punishment and on entering the company area we were surprised to find the company commander, Major Campbell-Baldwin; Sergeant Major Robinson; and platoon commander, Lieutenant E. C. Ellis; with Jimmy Davie and lots of others awaiting our arrival. We got quite a cheer on entering the company area. No mention was ever made of our assistance on the return journey.

Shortly after these events Jimmy Davie went on demobilisation; I was promoted to sergeant on 25th April 1946 and appointed No. 8 platoon sergeant, C company. The platoon was billeted in a large Dutch house on a hill with a crystal-clear stream running 50 feet below the house. This is where we had to do all our washing. There were no laundry facilities. From 6 p.m. to 6 a.m. two sentries were on duty for alternate 2-hour spells. I used to get up and check the sentries at various times to see that they were alert. At 1.30 a.m. one morning I found both sentries fast asleep. I roused the ones who were due on from 2 a.m. to 4 a.m. and then placed the two sleeping sentries under close arrest.

At 6 a.m. on the same morning I got up to find that all the washing that had been done on the previous day had vanished from the clothes lines. Among the washing were two jungle-green uniforms belonging to me. At 8 a.m. Sergeant Major Robinson marched the two sentries and myself in front of the company commander. After I had given evidence the company commander (who did not have the powers to deal with them on such a serious charge) remanded the two sentries to be dealt with by the commanding officer. The sergeant major then marched us out of the company commander's office and the two sentries were taken away. I was about to return to my platoon when the sergeant major said, 'Hold on a bit.' He then marched me in front of the company commander, and charged me with losing my kit by neglect. I could do nothing but plead guilty and had to hand over my pay book to the company commander, who entered in the cost of two jungle-green uniforms to be deducted from my future pay. By the look on Major Campbell-Baldwin's face I don't think he thought it a fair charge – and neither did I – but that was the army in those days.

A few days after this we had a visit from our brigadier who was based with 1 brigade at Tandjoer. On the morning following his visit C company were detailed to escort the brigadier from the Poentjak Pass back to Tandjoer, a distance of 20 miles. The road was jungle-clad most of the way, with endless hills and valleys and numerous hair pin bends. Half of No. 8 platoon were in the leading 3-ton truck while the remainder of the platoon followed in another 3-ton truck. Behind us came the brigadier and Major Campbell-Baldwin in a staff car followed by the remainder of the company. After travelling for about 10 miles we rounded a bend to find our way blocked by a massive tree. Everyone shot out of the vehicle, as did the occupants of the truck following us. The brigadier in the meantime, who had watched the troops vanishing from the trucks in front of him, turned to Major Campbell-Baldwin and said, 'Fine show, major.'

'Nothing like this has been arranged,' was the reply, 'there must be something more serious ahead.'

Lieutenant Ellis, the platoon commander, took half of the platoon down one side of the road and I took the other half down the other side of the road. We found that trees had been felled as far as we could see. After crawling under and over ten trees we were amazed to find that a complete section of the road 100 yards long and 3 feet deep had literally been shovelled into the valley overnight. We pressed on and found that another 50 trees had been felled beyond the massive gap in the road. No extremists were encountered. The brigadier and escort had to return to the Poentjak Pass. It was not a particularly difficult problem to clear away the trees but the gap in the road was a much more serious problem and was eventually solved by bringing up a Bailey Bridge from Jakarta.

My 21st birthday was spent with my platoon stationed on high vantage points overlooking some of the worst bends in the Poentjak Pass. The vantage points were manned regularly to ensure that the convoys of trucks got through to Bandoeng. One could see the convoy snaking its way up the pass, crawling along at 10 miles an hour, a beautiful target for extremists in ambush positions. When I went to the sergeants' mess that night I had my first alcoholic drink and first cigarette. There were three Mathiesons in the sergeants' mess – the sergeant major of A company, the regimental quartermaster sergeant and myself.

During our stay in the Poentjak Pass Major Campbell-Baldwin, the company commander, decided that an attempt would be made to climb the volcanic mountain, Mount Panga-ranga. He asked for volunteers to accompany him; 20 did so, including Sergeant Major Murdoch of D company, Sergeant Major Robinson of C company and myself. Initially we were faced with dense tropical forest but the going was not too bad, the incline being not too steep; and it was quite cool under the dense foliage. As we got higher and higher climbing became much more strenuous and the foliage began to thin out. About 1000 feet from the summit we came out on to a treeless area. By this time 14 of the volunteers intimated that they were unable to go any further. The remaining six struggled on and got to the rim of the crater 10 000 feet above sea level.

From the edge of the crater one looked down at least 500 feet into a bubbling cauldron of molten lava and sulphur. Three of the six who completed the climb were Major Campbell-Baldwin, Sergeant Major Murdoch and myself. I cannot remember the names of the other three. Near the top of the crater we came across a small unmanned meteorological station. I left a postcard in the met. station with the names of the six who had completed the climb.

In August 1946, with the continuing build-up of Dutch

troops who gradually took over the British commitments, our battalion was relieved by the Dutch and we moved back to Jakarta. This time we were accommodated in Dutch barracks at Meester Cornelis on the outskirts of Jakarta at the junction of the Bogor Bekassi roads. This turned out to be a historic coincidence.

Gallant forerunners

In 1811, 135 years before, the 78th Regiment of the Seaforth Highlanders had played the largest part in the defeat of a force of French troops twice the size of their own at Meester Cornelis. On 26th August 1811 the commanding officer of the 78th Regiment Seaforth Highlanders, Lieutenant Colonel William Campbell, was seriously wounded; he died of his wounds on 28th August. Officers and men of the 72nd Regiment Seaforth Highlanders were therefore in the right place at the right time to attend a memorial service for Lieutenant Colonel Campbell exactly 135 years after his death. It was held in the English church, Jakarta, on 28th August 1946. A historical note of what actually happened in 1811 reads as follows:

In 1811 the 78th Regiment went to Java as part of the expedition under Sir Samuel Auchmuty which was dispatched for the purpose of ejecting the French from the island, which was the property of the Dutch. This was during the Napoleonic wars. The landing took place at Tjilintjung about 2 miles east of Tandjoeng Priok. Batavia (the Dutch name for Jakarta) was captured without opposition on 8th August. The French had decided to retire to the health resort of Weltevreden and, from this salubrious spot, watch disease slowly but inevitably destroy their opponents' force in the pestilential precincts of Batavia. On the night of 9th/10th August the 1st Division (strength about that of the present-day brigade), of which the 78th formed a part, advanced on Weltevreden. It was found that an enemy division had retired to a strong position further south on the Cornelis road. One flank of this position was secured by an unbridged unfordable river and the other by the Sloka Canal. This made a frontal attack on the axis of the Cornelis road unavoidable. The Commander in Chief, Sir Samuel Auchmuty, wrote:

'This position was strong, defended by an abbatis, occupied by 3000 of their best troops and four guns of horse artillery. It was attacked with spirit and judgement, and, after an obstinate resistance, carried at the point of the bayonet. The enemy force was completely routed and their guns captured. In this action the British casualties were 91 killed and wounded. The enemy lost 300 men, 300 guns and a quantity of military stores in the arsenal at Weltevreden.'

The lines at Cornelis now confronting the British were no mere temporary defence works but a solid fortification constructed according to the latest military engineering technique. This was held by 10 000 unshaken troops and 280 cannon. Sir Samuel could muster little more than half that number of men. He was, however, able to bring up heavy artillery from the fleet by the Batavia–Weltevreden waterways and the navy played a distinguished part both with its guns and its pikes in the subsequent operations. The preparations for the attack took a considerable time, but by 24th August the British batteries were ready and they fired throughout the following day. The lines of Cornelis were attacked and carried on 26th August, and it was on this day that the commanding officer of the 78th Regiment Seaforth Highlanders received the wounds from which he died two days later.

After the action the Commander in Chief wrote:

'In the action of the 26th the numbers (of enemy) killed were immense, but it has been impossible to form an accurate statement of the amount. About 1000 have been buried in the works. Multitudes were cut down in the retreat, the rivers are choked up with the dead, and the huts and woods were filled with the wounded who have since expired. We have taken near 5000 prisoners; among them are three general officers, 34 field officers, 70 captains and 150 subaltern officers. The 78th Regiment lost one officer and 33 men killed and wounded in the action at Weltevreden and, in the action at Cornelis, their commanding officer and over 160 casualties. The French made another stand at Semarang where they were defeated on September 16th 1811. The 78th took part in this action. Two days later the unconditional surrender of Java was effected.'

The Regiment remained in Java until 1816 and were engaged against the rebellious Sultan of Djocjacarta in 1812. The capture of his stronghold resulted in much prize money for the troops. Two large silver soup tureens were purchased by the officers from the loot captured and are still in the officers' mess.

According to the records of the English church, Batavia, Lieutenant Colonel Campbell's grave was moved to its present site in 1913. The general post office was being rebuilt in 1913 and the ground at the rear of the GPO had to be cleared; and this was where Lieutenant Colonel Campbell was initially buried. His present place of rest is near a well in the midst of a few native houses. We found the tombstone in an excellent state of preservation. It had been used by the native women for washing their clothes on. The inscription on the tombstone reads as follows:

Here lies the remains of Lieutenant Colonel William Campbell of His Britannic Majesty's 78th Regiment, who died on the 28th August 1811 of wounds received on the 26th of that month while bravely leading on his regiment to attack the strongly fortified lines of Cornelis, defended by a gallant enemy. To him who living was beloved by all for his gentle manners, and his many virtues, who in death merited and received the applause of his country. To him the companion of many happy years and the father of her children, this frail memorial of unperishing regard is erected by his afflicted widow.

The 1st battalion of the Seaforth Highlanders, the 72nd Regiment, landed at Jakarta on the 28th September 1945 and on returning to Jakarta from the Poentjak Pass in August 1946 were billeted in the Dutch barracks about 500 yards east of where the action took place in 1811. Casualties suffered by the Ist battalion 1945/46 were two officers killed and three wounded, six other ranks killed and 22 wounded.

On our second visit to Jakarta we found that the town had livened up with the opening up of restaurants, etc. The town was full of young Dutch troops, some of whom were quite arrogant and a number of incidents occurred between the Dutch and soldiers from the battalion. One fight in the Black Cat restaurant between Seaforths and Dutch troops resulted in the Dutch owners of the restaurant painting a sign in red paint on one of the large plate glass windows: *Out of bounds to the Seaforth Highlanders.*

Since we'd first landed in Java all crates coming ashore containing food, soap, etc., had displayed a large sticker on the ends of the crates with the Union Jack and the words 'Buy British The Best'. After the incident at the Black Cat restaurant some unknown Seaforth got hold of one of the stickers and, after cutting out the words 'the best', stuck the label on the plate glass window which contained the Union Jack and Buy British. Under the words 'Buy British' he stuck a condom to the window and added the words, 'and f . . . the foreigner'.

On three occasions during our brief final stay in Jakarta I had to carry out 24-hour duties; two of these were at the Indian General Hospital and the third at Glodak Prison. These duties entailed guarding two soldiers from the battalion who had contracted syphilis and who had escaped from custody on five occasions during which they committed such offences as theft, burglary and serious assault. Their practice was to wait until their guards were inalert and then escape from the hospital, forcibly take over a passing taxi (pony and trap) and throw the owner off the vehicle. They would then commit the crimes to which I have referred and would end up in a seedy area of the town. As five noncommissioned officers had been reduced in rank through their escaping I made it clear to them when I was in charge of the guard that my men, consisting of a lance corporal and two soldiers, had explicit instructions that if they attempted to escape they would be shot. Furthermore, at 10 p.m. I saw to it that each man had one of his wrists handcuffed to his iron bedstead. I never dozed off on that particular duty. As they were responsible for so many noncommissioned officers being reduced in rank they were eventually incarcerated in the Glodak Prison, still under the watchful eye of a reduced guard. On our subsequent return to Malaya they were court-martialled and sentenced to 5 years' imprisonment; they were sent to Lucknow in India to do their time. When India received its independence in 1947 they were no doubt shipped back to the United Kingdom.

In mid-September 1946 our company commander, Major Campbell-Baldwin, was about to leave the battalion to attend staff college in the United Kingdom. When handing over the company to Major R. I. MacKenzie it was found that there was a discrepancy of 400 guilders in the President Regimental Institute (PRI) fund. Every company ran their own PRI fund – one of the duties of the company quartermaster sergeant. From the PRI, soldiers could buy razor blades, soap, toothpaste, boot polish, etc. With the continual movement of the battalion it is possible that some of the PRI stores had been mislaid or pilfered but as the company quartermaster sergeant was in sole charge of the PRI goods and cash, he was reduced to the rank of sergeant and I was promoted to acting colour sergeant. Major Campbell-Baldwin, however, had to make good the loss of 400 guilders, the equivalent of £53.7s.6d in sterling at that time. After a discussion with the three platoon officers it was agreed that when the platoons were next on parade they be told about the loss and that their company commander would have to make good the loss. At the same time a proposal would be put to the men that the company reimburse the company commander before he left the regiment and to do this the price of goods in the PRI stores would be increased by two or three cents. As Major Campbell-Baldwin was such a popular company commander the entire company agreed wholeheartedly with the proposal and I am glad to say that the money was repaid to the company commander before he left to attend staff college.

The total battle casualties suffered by the 23rd Indian Division from the 28th September 1945 until the end of October 1946 was as follows:

	Killed	Wounded	Missing	
Officers	21	41	4	
Viceroy, commissioned officers and Gurkha officers	9	35	2	
British, other ranks	7	27	3	
Indian, other ranks, and Gurkha, other ranks	370	705	153	
Total	407	808	162	(1377)

This was a dreadful loss of life for a peacetime period, particularly in view of the fact that 3 years later, in 1949, the Dutch pulled out of Indonesia.

Malaya

After exactly one year, on 28th September 1946, the 1st battalion Seaforth Highlanders embarked on the Dutch troopship *MV Klipfontein* to return to Malaya. After a 5-day journey we docked at Port Swettenham and moved to the state of Perak in North Malaya. C company was sent on detachment to Bidor and then to Kampar, two small towns 42 miles and 36 miles respectively from the capital, Ipoh. Our duties consisted mainly of retraining after a hectic year in Java which included route marches, regimental drill, map reading and operating with the police against people who were then called bandits (later to be known as communist terrorists). Other companies were detached throughout Perak State with headquarters and administrative companies being in Ipoh. In December 1946, prior to a move to Gillman Barracks, Singapore, the battalion came together again when we were billeted at Tanjong Rambutan 12 miles from Ipoh. We were in fact billeted inside an asylum. On New Year's Day 1947 a fancy dress football match was held between the officers' and sergeants' messes. This was normal practice in the battalion. The commanding officer was the goalkeeper for the officers and the regimental sergeant major for the sergeants. Tug Wilson was the RSM at the time and two officers onlooking at the rear of the RSM's goalposts, took a hold of him and handcuffed him to the goalpost. In another incident the commanding officer saved a good shot, held on to the ball, jumped into his jeep behind the goalposts, and drove up the pitch and between the sergeants' goalposts. The referee was a bugler who sounded defaulters during every foul (the noise being, therefore, almost continuous). Watching all this from their wired-in accommodation were Chinese, Indian, Malay and other inmates of the asylum.

On 3rd January 1947 the battalion left Tanjong Rambutan by rail for Singapore. Following the battalion's departure the superintendent in charge of the asylum had a deputation of inmates wanting to know why they could not be released as the crazy people who had been playing football a few days earlier had all gone. The superintendent must have found it rather difficult to give a convincing reply to that question. On arrival in Singapore we moved into Gillman barracks about 4 miles from the city centre. These were proper barracks for a battalion – nice, airy two-storey barrack blocks. Spit and polish, drills, company and battalion inspections and parades were the general order of the day.

The battalion was issued with sheets (bed linen) for the first time and, being a colour sergeant, I had a difficult time keeping a track on sheets with soldiers bartering or selling sheets, as well as shortages from the Chinese laundry. To survive as a colour sergeant you had to be as smart as the next person. Sheets for the laundry were tied up in bundles of ten and one counted the sheets from the front of the bundle where the sheets were folded over. It was possible to fold over the sheets in such a manner as to make it look as if there were ten in the bundle when there were only eight. This worked the same way if the laundry contractor discovered that he had been 'done' when accepting a definite number of sheets and found that there was a shortage. The battalion quartermaster at the time was Lieutenant Quartermaster Mills; called cushy Mills, he was anything but. He was an ex-regimental sergeant major and RSMs usually progressed from RSM to lieutenant quartermaster.

The battalion quartermaster would suddenly swoop on a company without warning and check their entire stores. On one particular day my clerk, Private Perry, a very bright Glaswegian, saw the quartermaster heading in our direction and warned me what was afoot. To survive as a colour sergeant in those days you always had to be on the lookout to win, pick up or otherwise amass items of kit and even furniture – no stealing. Extra items of kit such as bootlaces, all types of webbing, pouches, braces, belts and gaiters, were stored in identifiable boxes so that they could be moved in the event of a surprise check by the quartermaster. To be on the safe side, Perry and I moved our excess stores out of the storeroom. Sure enough, in walked Lieutenant Mills and demanded the G 1098 – stores ledger. He went through the ledger and we had to produce and count everything in front of him which was recorded in the ledger. It turned out that I was short of six pairs of bootlaces. He demanded my pay book and in red ink entered the cost of the six pairs of bootlaces to be deducted from my next pay. I could have produced 100 pairs of bootlaces but did not dare mention the fact.

On Saturday morning, once a month, the entire battalion was on parade and all the kit issued by the military was laid out on the beds in the barrack rooms for inspection. The uniforms of all men on parade were inspected by the commanding officer and if he was not satisfied with the state of dress he would tell the quartermaster to replace the tunic, trousers, balmoral, etc., at the next exchanges. The inspection of the ranks was carried out as follows: commanding officer accompanied by company commander, lieutenant quartermaster accompanied by company quartermaster, regimental sergeant major accompanied by the company sergeant major. When the commanding officer picked out something he told the quartermaster, who told the company quartermaster to make a note for exchanges the following Tuesday.

After the inspection of the battalion on parade every soldier had to stand by his bed for the barrack kit inspection. Same procedure: the commanding officer would condemn items of kit; the battalion quartermaster then ordered the company quartermaster to make a note of exchanges. After this parade and kit inspection I had pages of names and details of kit to be exchanged, and on the Tuesday following the inspections I paraded 50 men out of a company strength of 130 and marched them to the quartermaster's stores. They were lined up in single file and made their way to the open hatch in the side of the quartermaster's stores. The upshot was that very little was exchanged. A typical example was a soldier handing in his balmoral for exchange; the quartermaster had a look at it and threw it back to the soldier with the remark that it was good enough for another 6 months.

On 23rd March 1947 I was granted leave and left for the United Kingdom on SS *Ranchi*. The passage took 3 weeks and 1 day, the ship arriving at Tilbury Docks, London on 14th April 1947. Infantry sergeants were generally always detailed to be troop deck sergeants on board troopships. I had 250 troops on my designated deck space and all slept in hammocks. Reveille was at 6 a.m. and my job was to get all ranks out of their hammocks. Hammocks had to be rolled up showing the two blankets supplied and then stacked in the hammock racks provided. Corporals and lance corporals were then detailed to collect the breakfast from the galley and dish out the breakfast to the 18 soldiers at their individual tables. After breakfast all dixies, crockery and cutlery were returned to the galley and the clean up of the accommodation area commenced. At 11 a.m. every morning the ship's captain, accompanied by the troop commander and ship's regimental sergeant major, commenced a thorough inspection of the accommodation, shining torches in all the odd corners. After ship's inspection one could relax but was still responsible for organising the collection and distribution of meals throughout the day. It therefore worked out that one did not see the light of day until well after 11 a.m.

I was due to return to Malaya from Southampton on the 16th May and duly reported to the military transit camp at Southampton to be told that I had had my leave extended to 1 week, that this notification had been sent to my home and that after the week I had to report to Liverpool to get a troopship back to Malaya. I explained that I had not received the notification when I left Orkney and that it would take me a week to get to Orkney and back to Liverpool, travelling all the time. I asked that they either put me up in Southampton or I could move on to Liverpool. This was apparently out of the question. I was issued with a warrant from Southampton to Orkney and with another from Orkney to Liverpool.

I left Southampton on the Thursday evening and arrived in Thurso after the car-ferry *St Ola* (the only transport going to Orkney) had left at 12 midday on the Saturday. As there were no sailings on Sunday I had to wait until midday on Monday before getting across to Orkney. I was home on the Monday night and left at 7 a.m. on the Tuesday morning to cross with the *St Ola* from Stromness to Scrabster at 8.30 a.m. on my way to Liverpool. I booked into the transit camp at Liverpool and then went for a look around town.

I was walking up a wide street in the city and I noticed a major walking down the other side of the street. I heard a scream from the other side of the street: 'staff sergeant'. I made my way across the street through traffic and saluted the major. He then asked if I did not recognise the King's Commission. I said I did but thought it pointless saluting an officer who was at least 50 feet away and hidden at times by the passing traffic. He then asked for my number and name, which I supplied. He then wanted to know where I was stationed and when I said Gillman barracks, Singapore, you could see the disappointment on his face. This officer was the type of idiot who had never been anywhere, had no medals and gave the army a bad name.

I embarked on the troopship *Empress of Scotland* on the 23rd May. At this time shirts and ties with the lapels of the tunic turned down were all the go in the army. After getting on board at Liverpool, all sergeants, colour sergeants and sergeant majors were mustered by the ship's RSM. He obviously did not approve of the new dress style and every senior noncommissioned officer who wore a tie was earmarked for ship's duties. I was one of those and was detailed for duty as ship's police. This entailed 6 hours on duty in every 24 hours. The duties were to enforce no smoking in unauthorised areas, fire duties and making sure that other ranks did not encroach or stray into the confines of officers' or female military accommodation areas.

On disembarking at Singapore on 11th June 1947 I reported to Gillman barracks to find that C company had in the meantime been detached to Glugor barracks, Penang Island, to train locally-enlisted personnel. My job as colour sergeant was to organise the clothing, feeding and paying of all ranks in C company and the local recruits. C company was accommodated in the barrack blocks of Glugor barracks. The local recruits were in tented accommodation. During this period I was asked by the company commander and the commanding officer whether I wished to become an officer in the regiment and told that, if so, I had first of all to pass battalion and brigade examinations. I thought I would give it a try, along with Sergeant Griffin. We passed our examinations and were accepted as potential candidates. We were then called in by the commanding officer to be told that we were to be sent to Lucknow in India to attend an officer cadet training unit for 6 months, but before we went we would have to sign on for a further 3 years. As I was in No. 62 release group and due to be demobilised in November 1947, and as I had domestic problems at home, I decided against the offer. Sergeant Griffin did likewise.

In early October 1947 I moved back to Gillman barracks, Singapore, prior to release from the army. On 10th October 1947 Major Swinton Lee, second in command of the battalion, signed my discharge papers; very sadly, he was killed a few days later when he was thrown from his horse in Singapore. On the morning of the 15th October those going on demobilisation – about 20 in group 62 – were paraded at the guard room at the main gate to the barracks. Along came Lieutenant Colonel Jock Douglas, the commanding officer. He shook hands with everyone and when speaking to me said that it was still not too late to change my mind if I wished to reconsider becoming an officer. I explained that I had domestic problems to sort out and that although I enjoyed the service my domestic problems had to have priority.

From Gillman barracks we were transported to Nee Soon transit camp and 3 days later boarded *MV Sloterdyck*, a Dutch freighter converted into a troopship. There were 3000 troops on board. Sleeping accommodation was very cramped. Bunks were of the folding type, five tiers high. Feeding was well organised. Everyone went to the galley and picked up a segmented tray with sections for soup, main meal and sweet, which were dished up in a fast-moving queue. The ablutions were very crude. In the centre of the ship there were 72 toilets and 72 wash basins – 36 toilets along one side of the ship and 36 on the other. In the centre of the ablution area there were two rows of 36 wash basins, back-to-back. There were no seats on the toilets and no partitions between the toilets – just two open rows of 36 porcelain toilets. One morning a sergeant from Orkney who was in the army education service was sitting on a toilet beside me. He was reading a book which he held in one hand and he had a razor in the other hand. He put out his hand holding the razor to get some toilet paper and at that moment his neighbour sat down on his arm. The sergeant's hand automatically opened with the result that his razor disappeared down the toilet and was washed away by the continuous stream of salt water that rushed through the main pipe. After an otherwise uneventful journey the *MV Sloterdyck* docked at Tilbury, London. Hailing from the north, I had to report to York to get fitted out with civilian clothing. I then returned home to the Orkney Islands.

IV

Civvy Street

After two weeks' leave I took up employment as a haulage driver with a local company. The business had run down completely due to the cost of repairs to the two ailing haulage vehicles owned by the company. When I was asked to try and get business moving again I was told to pick up one vehicle from a garage in Holm; the other was under repair in a garage in St Margarets Hope. We did get a contract to remove old barbed wire entanglements, scrap metal, etc., from Hoxa Head, South Ronaldsay, and deliver the scrap to Hatston Aerodrome, Kirkwall. Both vehicles were available by then. One, a Morris Commercial flat bed without tipper, was mainly used for transporting cattle and sheep to the auction market. The other was a short-wheelbase Fordson with tipper. I used the tipper for the work at Hoxa Head and every morning picked up a squad of Italian prisoners from the island of Flotta under a British foreman and took them to Hoxa Head. The trouble with this vehicle was that, after it had travelled 5 miles, the radiator would boil and the rubber cap on the radiator shoot into the air, covering the windscreen with steam. When this happened, which was regularly, I had to stop, let the engine cool down and refill the radiator. I carried a 5-gallon drum of water for this purpose. Normally, three stops were made on a trip from South Ronaldsay to Kirkwall in order to avoid this problem. Eventually the engine seized up and I had to use the Morris Commercial.

One day in early March 1948 I had just got to the top of a hill at Hoxa Head and was driving down to the parking area at the bottom of the hill (where there were steep cliffs and a drop into the sea). I put my foot on the brake; nothing happened. I changed down; nothing happened. I pulled on the handbrake; nothing happened. In the meantime the truck was gaining speed and the Italians in the back of the vehicle were banging on the roof. The foreman sitting beside me in the cab asked what was wrong. I told him I had no idea. I had tried everything. Fortunately at the bottom of the hill there was a wide turn into a large parking area, only 50 feet from the cliffs. I managed to turn into the parking area without turning the vehicle over. The vehicle ran up a slight incline and came to a stop. I jumped out of the cab and was astonished to find that the offside rear double wheels, complete with half shaft, had moved at least 15 inches out from the axle. Apparently the lock nuts had broken, allowing the half shaft (complete with double wheels) to move out from the crown wheel, thereby disengaging gears, severing brake pipes, etc. Although one of the shareholders of the company offered to buy me a new vehicle, to be paid off as and when I could, I did not take up the offer.

That was the end of that haulage company and I went to work at the Lyness Naval Base on the island of Hoy. After working in a naval base workshop which repaired and maintained cranes I was asked if I was interested in taking up crane driving. I was delighted with the offer and was trained by a great crane driver, Jimmy Sinclair from Crock Ness, Longhope. The crane I normally used was the Grafton crane with a 50-foot jib mainly used for unloading coal boats with a grab. The biggest problem with the Grafton crane was keeping the steam up. When I became proficient at handling the crane the workers on the docks and on board the ships were keen for competition. On one particular day a coal boat was ready in the morning with 800 tons to be unloaded – 400 tons in each hold. Jimmy Sinclair was on the one hold and I had the other. Initially it was a case of work for the crane driver only: dropping the grab, bringing the load ashore and loading lorries or, if none were there, dropping the load on the quayside. When one got to the sole of the ship two men were in the hold guiding the grab and one on the deck signalling when to drop it. On this occasion I beat my instructor, to the delight of my crew. Jimmy Sinclair was also pleased and congratulated me on the handling of the crane.

As the work at Lyness was getting less and the majority of the permanent staff were being offered jobs at Rosyth Naval Dockyard and further afield, I was glad to hear from my brother Peter, in early August 1948, that there was a job going at St Margarets Hope, where an extension to the school was being built. The contract had been awarded to Orkney Builders Ltd., and I joined my brother and two other workers. Initially we had to clear a foundation for the extension, which meant moving a large quantity of clay 3 feet deep with pick, shovel and barrow. After working on this for about 10 days in very wet weather, my brother and I went to lunch at my mother's house. At 1 o'clock on this particular day there was an appeal on the radio for volunteers to join the Malayan Police as sergeants on contract for 2 years. Anyone who had held the rank of sergeant or above in the services could apply.

I returned to work that afternoon and it started to pour with rain. At about 3 o'clock in the afternoon I was wheeling a barrow of clay up a plank. I stopped, tipped the barrow off the plank, and said to my brother, 'There's no future in this; I am going to join the Malayan Police', and walked off the job. I had always wanted to return to Malaya as I loved the country and the people.

I wrote to the Crown Agents in London and by return received a telegram stating that I should report to them for an interview. I had my interview, and was told to return home and that I would get my interview result shortly. Before I got

46

home a telegram arrived saying that I had been selected and that a plane would be leaving Hounslow Airport, London, on 2nd September and they would like to see me there. It was essential, however, to complete a passport application form and forward the same to the Crown Agents for action. I obtained the form. In 1948 one had to obtain the signatures of two people who knew you well and they had to be a JP, bank manager or minister of religion.

Herbert MacKenzie, a watchmaker by trade, was the local JP. He was well known to everyone and was a very popular man. He knew my family well and had no hesitation in signing the form. As I did not know the bank manager I went to see the family minister, the Revd James Cameron Steen. When I explained the reason for my visit he completely refused to sign the form, saying that if he signed it he would be signing my death warrant. As it turned out he was almost right. He then told me that he knew the Chief Constable of the Liverpool City Police very well and he was sure that he could get me into that force. I told him that I was too short to be accepted in any force in the United Kingdom (5ft 7in.) and that there was no point in pursuing that line. I asked him again to sign the form which he refused to do.

Two nights later I returned to the manse and tried again. Knowing that the minister was partial to a drop of whisky, I went armed with a half bottle. I explained that time was getting short, that I was determined to go and that in no way should he himself feel responsible if anything happened to me. He finally agreed to sign the passport application form. After he had signed I produced the half bottle and we had a pleasant farewell drink.

V

Malayan Police Force

It is necessary to explain why the Malayan Government was so desperate for the services of ex-Palestine police and ex-sergeants out of the services. It was the result of a long-term aim of the Malayan Communist Party to take over Malaya by force of arms. Communism was first established in Malaya and Singapore (mainly Singapore) in 1927 in the form of the Nanyang (South Seas) Communist Party. At a secret meeting in 1930 the Nanyang Communist Party was dissolved and the Malayan Communist Party formed. At this meeting it was decided to work for the establishment of a communist republic in Malaya under the control of Moscow. From 1930 to 1939 the Malayan Communist Party which never registered as a political organisation, and was therefore an illegal body, promoted strikes and labour troubles on rubber estates, tin mines and in all other industries. In 1937 the inspector general of police admitted that the country had passed through the most serious crisis in its history and had almost succumbed to communist intrigue.

In August 1939, after the non-aggression pact between Germany and Russia, the Malayan Communist Party took its orders from Moscow and opposed the war against Germany. The party then launched a violent anti-British campaign, followed by waves of strikes which all but brought the production of rubber and tin to a standstill. In June 1941, although the

German attack on Russia threw the party into confusion, it obeyed an order from Moscow to cooperate with Britain. The party ceased calling strikes and fomenting labour troubles. A few days after the Japanese attack on Malaya in December 1941 the secretary general of the Malayan Communist Party sent a message to the government offering unconditional cooperation against the common enemy. In view of the new relationship between Russia and Britain, the government could do nothing but accept the Party's offer, which included the offer of its members as a resistance force behind the Japanese lines. About 200 communists were trained in guerilla warfare. However, the speed of the Japanese race down the Malayan peninsula prevented the guerillas from being satisfactorily equipped with explosives and wireless transmitters for communication with allied headquarters.

During the Japanese occupation the communist guerillas called themselves the Malayan People's Anti-Japanese Army (MPAJA), and they grew in strength as hundreds of young Chinese rubber tappers, tin miners and others joined them in order to fight the Japanese. The MPAJA units were never a serious menace to the Japanese, being ill equipped for the job. In 1943 the executive of the Malayan Communist Party, confident that the war would be won by the allies, drew up plans for establishing a soviet type republic in Malaya immediately after the defeat of Japan. The ready-made MPAJA would become the national army of liberation. A party order instructed commanders to expand their units and prepare them for the liberation of the oppressed people of Malaya by direct action against the British at the end of the Japanese war.

From May 1943 onwards a considerable number of allied guerillas (known as Force 136) were parachuted into Malaya or landed by submarine from India and Ceylon in preparation for an allied invasion. With them came supplies of the latest weapons. They joined Chinese guerilla units, trained them in the art of ambush, attack and jungle warfare. By the beginning

49

of August 1945 the MPAJA was believed to be about 7000 strong.

Following the dropping of the atomic bombs on Hiroshima and Nagasaki on 6th August 1945 the Japanese surrendered unconditionally on 14th August 1945. The sudden surrender of the Japanese took the allies by surprise and there was a lapse of time before allied troops arrived in Malaya. As soon as the Japanese surrendered the MPAJA emerged from the jungle wearing British uniforms and accepted tribute as the glorious anti-Japanese army. They took control of villages and towns, raised their three-starred flags and in general terrorised the people. The arrival of three divisions of allied troops stopped the Malayan Communist Party from launching an immediate revolt. The communist executive accepted a British order for the disbandment of the MPAJA. Guerillas were demobilised and paid gratuities, while their leader, Chin Peng, was subsequently awarded the OBE. The Malayan Communist Party instructed all its members in the MPAJA to set up and join the Malayan People's Anti-Japanese Army Old Comrades' Association in every village and town so that they would not be lost sight of. Funds paid into the association were used to feed, clothe and maintain a secret force which remained in the jungle.

The Malayan Communist Party, although thwarted from taking over the country in 1945, were by no means finished and immediately started forming trade unions and infiltrating other unions sponsored by government. By early 1948 they controlled practically all trade unions in Malaya as a result of which there were endless strikes, mainly due to intimidation. In April 1948 there were six shootings in this connection. On 31st May 1948 the government passed legislation restricting office bearers of trade unions from holding office unless they had at least 3 years' service in the industry concerned. Those convicted of extortion, intimidation and other similar crimes likewise could not hold office. The communist-dominated unions refused to comply with the new legislation and, fearing arrest and banishment, the leaders went underground.

During the first 2 weeks of June 1948 a large number of incidents directed at rubber estates and tin mines were carried out by communist terrorists, culminating in the murder of three European rubber planters and two Chinese planters on 16th June 1948. This resulted in a state of emergency being declared and the banning of the Malayan Communist Party. As the rubber estates and tin mines were the economic backbone of the country, which the communists intended to wreck, the government decided that these industries must be protected at all costs. So a special constabulary of 37 500 (mainly Malays) was raised under the government's emergency regulations. Some 500 British police sergeants were recruited to train the constabulary, and that is where I came in.

Facts and figures, Malaya, 1948

At this point it is necessary to say a little about the geography and climate of this lovely country. Malaya[1] is a peninsula running for 400 miles from the Thailand border south-east to the Indonesian islands. Its greatest width is 200 miles. Its area, 53 240 square miles, is a little larger than England without Wales. The southern extremity of the peninsula is only one and a half degrees north of the equator. The peninsula has a backbone of jungle-covered mountains rising to a height of 7000 feet, with an average height of between 2000 and 4000 feet. Four-fifths of the country is covered with dense tropical jungle. A hundred feet above the ground the trees make a solid roof of green shutting out the sky. From their branches curtains of vine and creeper join the undergrowth to make a jungle so dense that even an elephant may be difficult to distinguish at 25 yards, let alone a man in a jungle-green uniform.

When flying over such country, nothing can be seen below tree-top level. Even a large scale terrorist camp with a parade ground will remain invisible owing to the way the smaller trees thin out without disturbing the main canopy formed by the

[1]Now more commonly known as the Malay peninsula, part of Malaysia.

51

larger trees. The remaining one-fifth of the country, which has been developed, consists of rubber plantations, palm oil plantations, pineapple estates, rice fields, tin mines, villages and towns. The country lying to the west of the mountain range is far more highly developed than that lying to the east.

The rivers of Malaya are numerous and have played a big part in the early development of the lower-lying country. In many areas they remain the primary means of communication for the inhabitants of the numerous picturesque Malay villages which dot their banks. Clear and swift-flowing in their upper reaches, they tend to become sluggish and muddy in colour on their way through the plains. On the west coast dense mangrove usually surround their entrance to the sea, but the east coast, with its long unbroken stretches of sand and surf, provides a beautiful and more fitting end to these important features of the life of the Malay rural community.

At the southern tip of the peninsula lies the island of Singapore, joined to the peninsula by a road and rail causeway three-quarters of a mile long. The principal features of the Malayan climate are copious rainfall, high humidity and uniform temperature. The year is divided into the south-west and north-east monsoon seasons, which correspond roughly with the summer and winter of northern latitudes. Rainfall averages 100 inches a year though certain areas average as much as 198 and as little as 65 inches a year. The average maximum temperature in the plains is rather less than 90°F and the minimum 70°F. At the hill stations temperatures are considerably lower. The population of Malaya in 1950 was as follows: Malay, over 2 500 000; Chinese, just over 2 000 000; Indians and Pakistanis, over 500 000; Europeans and all others, 71 000. The main products of Malaya are rubber, tin, palm oil, coconuts (copra), pineapples, tea, gutta percha, manila hemp, jute and cocoa.

As I have already mentioned, on 2nd September 1948 I was appointed a police sergeant in the Special Constabulary, Federation of Malaya Police Force. I travelled to Malaya in a converted York bomber from Hounslow Airport, London, to Singapore, calling en route at Nicosia (Cyprus), Damascus, Bahrein, Karachi and Calcutta. Seating in the four-engined bomber consisted of webbing straps. This was anything but comfortable; when you sat down the person next to you shot up and when you leaned back your companion alongside shot forwards. The stops were for refuelling only so after 72 hours with no real breaks we arrived in Singapore. There were 60 sergeants on the flight.

On arriving in Singapore we were billeted in the Nee Soon transit camp. After a rest of 3 days in Singapore we were distributed throughout the Federation. Six of us proceeded by rail to Kuala Lumpur, the capital, and from there to Klang where we were informed of our destination. All six were posted to the Kuala Selangor District of Selangor State. I was paired with Sergeant Andrew MacLean, ex-Palestine Police. We were known as Group 14 in the special constabulary and our task was to train 150 special constables to guard Selangor Bulk Oil Installation and the following estates: Berjuntai, Strathmore, St Andrews, Holmwood, Sungei Rambai, Kampong Bahru and Sungei Selangor. Sergeant MacLean and I were billeted in an assistant manager's bungalow on Sungei Rambai estate. The estate manager was Jimmy Wilkie who came from Dunfermline in Scotland.

To carry out our duties each group of estates, which was run by two sergeants, was allocated a new Austin A40 car. Andrew MacLean and I got on very well together. He did most of the paper work such as drawing up duty rosters for all the estates and installations under our jurisdiction, measuring and ordering up uniforms, keeping a check on all firearms and ammunition issued and reporting to the officer in charge of the police district when ammunition was expended (all empty cartridges were returned to prove that this had happened). He also carried out a certain amount of training. As I was fresh out of the army I did most of the training, which included foot drill, stripping and assembling of weapons and hand grenades, firing on the range, physical training and fieldcraft. Drill in my opinion was considered absolutely necessary to instil discipline into this new force of men.

At least 90 per cent of special constables recruited were local Malays from Malay villages, rubber estates and small holdings. It was quite difficult initially to train these men due to the language barrier. I had picked up a smattering of Malay during military service, which was of some assistance, and on occasions we were fortunate enough to get the services of an English-speaking Malay corporal. When the corporal was not available the various drill movements were given by demonstration. On the whole the Malays loved drill, were keen to learn and were not difficult to train. They also had a great sense of humour. The officer in charge of the Kuala Selangor police district at the time was Mohamed Ariffin, assistant superintendent of police, a local Malay. He had been wounded by terrorists in 1946 and had a limp. He was an excellent boss, had a great sense of humour and was very popular in the district.

Two Turbulent Years

Things were going along fine until the morning of 15th December 1948 when four special constables from Sungei Selangor estate were making their way to Kampong Bahru estate for training. They were ambushed by communist terrorists when walking along the track which joined the two estates. All four special constables were killed and the terrorists got away with four rifles and 200 rounds of ammunition. The undergrowth on both Kampong Bahru and Sungei Selangor estates had got out of control during the Japanese occupation and due to a shortage of cash little could be done to slash it down during the 3 years following the surrender of the Japanese. Small strips were cleared in the line of the rubber trees to enable the tappers to get on with their work; elsewhere in the rubber estates the undergrowth was 4 to 5 feet tall, ideal cover for terrorists. Nine Chinese rubber tappers, suspected of aiding the terrorists, were arrested on Sungei Selangor estate after the ambush.

As a result of this ambush the remaining special constables on Sungei Selangor and Kampong Bahru estates quite naturally became jittery, and concern was also felt for the safety of the manager and assistant manager, both of whom lived on the Kampong Bahru estate. The two estates, owned by the Fesq family (French), were across the Selangor River. The only access to the estates was by sampan (Malay boat). The estates had no electricity and no telephone or radio communication. As a result, on 22nd December 1948 the officer in charge of the police district posted me to Kampong Bahru estate as a morale booster. I was welcomed by John Fesq, the manager of both estates, and his assistant John Cuthill, who hailed from Edinburgh.

During the few weeks I was at Kampong Bahru I carried out extensive training, including dummy attacks on the manager's bungalow, and organised general alarm systems. The special constables' guard duties consisted of 4 hours on and 8 hours off. To find out what it was like to do a 4-hour stint in a defence post, I frequently did 4 hours with the guards on duty. Four hours is a long period in the middle of the night in a pitch-black rubber estate and it was not surprising that occasionally a guard would let off a round or two at fireflies. When you have been staring into the inky blackness for a number of hours and you suddenly see tiny pin pricks of light in the distance it is possible for the unenlightened person to assume that it is people moving through the rubber with torches.

During my pleasant stay with John Fesq and John Cuthill I frequently went out with them plus two special constables at 6 a.m. in the morning – the time when work started on the estates. First there was a roll call of the workers and they were then sent to their various tasks. It was still dark at 6 a.m. and a particularly dangerous time for managers because communist terrorists could infiltrate the ranks of the workers during the roll call. As soon as daylight came, at around 6.30, the tappers moved off to their allocated tasks to tap the rubber trees. The manager and his assistant would cover quite a number of miles, checking on tapping, the slashing down of the undergrowth, the growth of new rubber trees and the cutting down of old rubber trees no longer producing an economic quantity of rubber. This daily task went on from 6 a.m. to 11 a.m. The special constables and I acted as guards to the management team during this difficult period. From time to time we also laid ambushes on likely tracks and searched squatter areas adjoining the estates.

Light relief

Two amusing incidents worthy of note occurred during my stay at Kampong Bahru. One evening John Fesq, John Cuthill and I were having a meal on the verandah of the wooden bungalow. Suddenly there was a rattle like a burst of machine gun fire. John Fesq immediately blew out the only light we had, an oil lamp, and everyone hit the floor. As we always carried our weapons with us, I picked up my sten gun and made my way to the defence post at the main gate to the bungalow. I asked the constables on duty what the noise was. They laughed and said that a rotten branch had become detached from a rubber tree and on its way down had hit other branches which made a sound like that of someone opening up with a machine gun. I was pleased to note that the constables had it all worked out.

A short time later we were again having a meal in the same circumstances when there was a loud explosion at the rear of the bungalow. Same procedure; light blown out, weapons picked up and we quietly made our way to the rear of the bungalow where the kitchen was situated. The regular Tamil cook was off sick at the time and a young Tamil boy was doing the cooking. He had a tin of sausages in a pot of boiling water and had omitted to puncture the tin, with the result that the tin of sausages and pot were blown to pieces. Thankfully the lad was uninjured. He certainly got a fright.

On 3rd January 1949 a field telephone line was erected between Kampong Bahru estate and Selangor River estate on the other side of the river; this meant that we were no longer cut off from the rest of civilisation and could call for assistance in an emergency. From this time until 8th February 1949 four reports were received of terrorists having been seen in and around the Sungei Selangor and Kampong Bahru estates.

The first report received was at 7.15 a.m on 11th January when a foreman from Sungei Selangor estate reported seeing 24 armed terrorists moving along the Sungei Selangor/Avondale estate boundary at 6 p.m. the previous evening. The information came too late for any action to be taken. At 10 a.m. on the morning of 11th January after I'd arrived at Sungei Selangor estate with the manager, assistant manager and two special constables we were informed by a foreman from Kampong Bahru estate who came riding after us on a bicycle that he and a number of his labourers had seen 30 armed terrorists about 10 minutes previously on the Inchamaram/Kampong Bahru estate boundary. We immediately proceeded to Riverside estate to inform the Scots Guards who were preparing to move off on patrol. We all proceeded by truck along the Raja Musa road to the boundary drain which separated the Inchamaram and Kampong Bahru estates. Proceeding down the path alongside the drain we came across two squatters' huts on our right, which were searched. One of the huts was empty but food was cooking. The platoon commander of the Scots Guards, 2nd Lieutenant Angus Ogilvie, left a few men in the hut with instructions to arrest the occupants if and when they returned. In the other hut were two men and two children, market gardeners and quite harmless. Their identity cards were in order. No contact was made with the terrorists.

On the morning of 1st February six constables and I laid

an ambush on a path on the boundary of Sungei Selangor and Inchamaram estates. The ambush was laid from 6 a.m. to 8.40 a.m. – no one approached. It had been reported to me on the previous evening that seven armed terrorists had been seen on the path 24 hours earlier.

In the afternoon (1st February) a Tamil coolie reported that he had seen a Chinese man dressed as a tapper armed with a sten gun at 5.15 p.m. moving south through the rubber on Sungei Selangor estate. I took three special constables and the Tamil coolie to the area where the terrorist had last been seen. The Tamil informant showed us the direction in which the terrorist had been heading; this turned out to be towards a kongsi (living accommodation of the Chinese tappers who worked on Sungei Selangor estate). We moved on to the kongsi and after positioning my special constables to cover the building I entered the building and searched every room – to no avail. From there we went back and made a thorough search of the area in which the terrorist had last been seen – without result. By this time it was pitch black in the rubber estate so we made our way back to Kampong Bahru estate.

On 6th February I was notified by the officer in charge of the Kuala Selangor police district that I was being transferred back to Sungei Rambai estate. I notified John Fesq that I would be leaving at 8 a.m. on 8th February. On 9th February, on my return to Sungei Rambai estate, I received the following letter from John Fesq:

Kampong Kuantan Estate,
Bukit Rotan P.O.
8th Feb 49

Dear Jock,
I have worked out the mess bill for January and after deducting 15 dollars for your laundry, which you had done outside, your bill comes to 114 dollars 53 cents. I hope that this figure will not shake you too much. I personally expected

it to be a good deal lower but the shopkeepers would not agree.

I am very sorry that you have now left us and I would like to take this chance to tell you how glad I was that you came to help us in Kampong Bahru and to thank you for the amount of trouble and hard work you put into it.

Yours sincerely,

John

The Kampong Kuantan estate given in the address was another estate owned by the Fesq family; John Fesq's father lived there.

Shortly after I returned to Sungei Rambai estate a lallang (long grass) fire broke out on the boundary of Sungei Rambai estate; and in police districts like Kuala Selangor the police were responsible for fire-fighting. Jimmy Wilkie, the manager of the estate, contacted the Kuala Selangor police station and a police jeep was dispatched towing a fire pump. Sergeant MacLean and I were notified at the same time and we proceeded to the fire. The police fire-fighters (constables) turned up in record time and ran out the hoses. There was seldom if ever any shortage of water in Malaya owing to the numerous rivers, streams and monsoon ditches throughout the country – and in this case there was a suitable monsoon ditch nearby with ample water. However, after no end of coaxing the pump would not start. The fire was creeping nearer to the estate all the time and if not stopped would burn down a large recently-planted section of rubber trees. Jimmy Wilkie, who was becoming very agitated, vanished, and he must have contacted the Kuala Selangor police station again to complain that the pump would not start. We were trying everything to get it going when on the scene came the officer in charge of the police district, Mohamed Ariffin. Jimmy Wilkie complained to the OCPD about the state of affairs and pointed out the serious loss that would occur if the fire was not put out. Mohamed Ariffin, looking at the pump and the sweating constables, said, in a quiet voice, 'She is a tired old lady.' Fortunately, after

59

further efforts, the pump did jump into life and the fire was extinguished before it could reach the young rubber trees. This was typical of Mohamed Ariffin; he never panicked, and spoke to people in such a way that no matter how mad or agitated they were the wind was taken out of their sails and they calmed down. Shortly after the lallang fire I was sent on a 2-week jungle training course at Kuala Kubu Bahru. The training camp was run by the 1st battalion Scots Guards. One sergeant from each group of estates was sent and when that sergeant returned the other sergeant went on the next course.

Occasionally we would go to Klang or Kuala Lumpur on a recreation run to the cinema or have a meal out. One Saturday evening four of us set off in Roy Seymour and Jock Keen's Austin A40. Before departing we disconnected the speedometer and put petrol in the tank. For duty runs we had to fill up a log book and we were not officially allowed to use the vehicle for recreational purposes. However, our superiors obviously felt that we were due some recreation and turned a blind eye to the occasional misuse of official transport. After having a drink with the manager of Bukit Rotan estate we set off for Klang, 26 miles away, to see a film show. Roy Seymour was driving. When negotiating a sharp bend he lost control of the car and hit three concrete markers on the bend. Damage to the vehicle was fairly extensive – radiator grill pushed in, nearside wing badly buckled, bumper twisted, wheel bent and tyre punctured. We manually pulled out the bumper and the grill, removed the damaged wheel and replaced it with the spare. On reaching Klang we went to a Chinese garage and told the owner to repair the vehicle in time for collection on Sunday evening. We had to stay in Klang overnight and returned to Kuala Selangor by bus early on Sunday morning. On Sunday evening Roy travelled back to Klang by bus to pick up the car. It was ready. He was then told that the chassis of the vehicle had also been damaged in the accident (cracked) but that this had been welded. Roy paid for the repairs and returned to his base at Selangor River estate. Almost a month later Roy and Jock Keen were at the Kuala Selangor police station seeing the officer in charge of the police district, Mohamed Ariffin. When leaving, the OCPD came out with them and, when chatting at the car, got down on his hands and knees, had a look under the car and said: 'They didn't make a bad job of it did they, Roy?' His intelligence network was pretty good. Shortly after that episode Mohamed Ariffin was transferred to the criminal investigation department at Campbell Road police station, Kuala Lumpur. His place was taken by Tim Hatton, assistant superintendent of the police.

A day to remember

A few days after Tim Hatton had taken over the district I received a telephone call from him in the early morning saying that terrorists had entered Berjuntai estate at 7 a.m. that morning from the surrounding jungle; they had herded all the rubber tappers together and relieved them of their identity cards, putting these in a pile and burning them. I was asked to look into the incident. With ten special constables I set off for Berjuntai estate and after questioning a number of tappers and obtaining information as to the terrorists' direction of departure, we set off in pursuit. They had disappeared to the rear of the estate, and here we came upon a trace cut in the jungle for about a mile, possibly done by ordnance survey staff. We moved along the trace noting occasional footprints and broken twigs. At the end of the trace we came up against secondary jungle, very difficult to negotiate. We were following what looked like tracks and after travelling for about half a mile came upon a small basha (hut) capable of accommodating six people.

The basha was constructed of poles cut from the jungle. The roof and three walls, rear and both sides, were made of attap (palm fronds) with the front open. The floor was constructed of split bamboo raised about a foot off the ground. There was no sign of any cooking having taken place. It appeared therefore that the terrorists had spent the previous

61

evening in the basha, then moved to the estate at dawn, relieved the tappers of their identity cards and returned the same way to their main camp somewhere in the Batu Arang forest reserve.

I decided to carry on further, but without a map and compass – not issued in the early days of the emergency – we were in danger of becoming lost. Again, in the early days of the emergency no rations were issued and not one of us had anything to eat. With the trees being so high it was only occasionally that one got a glimpse of the sun to work out a rough direction. Fortunately there were plenty of streams with cold, clear running water. At about 4 p.m. we were still stuck in the secondary jungle. I asked for a volunteer to climb a tree and told whoever volunteered that he should see smoke somewhere ahead, I hoped, which would be the Batu Arang coalfields. A Pakistani special constable from Sungei Rambai estate climbed the tree and with great excitement stated that he could see moshi (smoke) about 2 miles ahead. We carried on as fast as possible before darkness closed in – usually 6.30–7 p.m. At 6.15 p.m. we emerged from the jungle, and, knowing that the Scots Guards were stationed at Batu Arang and were not expecting us, had to move cautiously. After 15 minutes we saw a defence post in the distance, hailed the occupants and identified ourselves.

We were picked up by the Scots Guards and taken to the house of the two British police sergeants who were stationed at Batu Arang. My men were looked after by the local special constables. I received a most welcome mug of sweet black coffee from one of the sergeants which was like nectar. I don't believe that I have ever appreciated anything more in my life. I had had nothing to eat or drink, except water, from 7 a.m. to 7 p.m. I then telephoned Tim Hatton and told him where I was. He said, 'That is impossible, you couldn't do that distance in that time!' Well, we had. He sent out a police vehicle to take us back to Kuala Selangor.

On 6th May 1949 a report was received that terrorists had been seen in the Ijok area. I was requested to take a section of special constables and check the area. After patrolling the squatter area we entered the jungle behind it. Then, after travelling abut 500 yards, one of the constables tripped on a wire which set off an alarm. The alarm consisted of tins tied to a trip wire which surrounded an area of the jungle. Initially we thought this could be a terrorist camp although they were generally more sophisticated with their defences. After moving forwards a further 200 yards we came upon an illicit still for making samsu (rice wine). There was a cache of 500 gallons, all stored in glass carboys. There was only one Chinese male in the area, and he was immediately arrested. All carboys of the illicit samsu were smashed except one which was kept as evidence.

The Ijok area is 25 miles from Kuala Selangor and transport was waiting on the main road to take us back. The transport was a 15 cwt chevrolet truck with open back. It was dark when we left the squatter area with torrential rain. The Malay special constables in the rear of the truck naturally got soaked and apparently, without my knowledge, one of them decided to sample the samsu on the way back. On arriving at Kuala Selangor police station I unhooked the rear door of the truck to let the special constables disembark. One special constable stood at the rear of the vehicle with his rifle and fell like a stone flat on his face. This was the constable who had sampled the illicit samsu. Powerful stuff. He, of course, had to be disciplined. The arrested Chinese male was handed over to the customs authorities for prosecution.

During mid-May 1949 it was decided that the three groups of estates in Kuala Selangor district should set up a training camp at the Selangor Bulk Oil Installation to which 30 special constables would be sent for 3 weeks' intensive training before returning to their respective estates. Then there would be further intakes of 30 until we had covered all 450 special constables in the three groups. Sergeant MacLean and I were known as group 14, Sergeant Jock Keen and Roy Seymour group 13 and Sergeant Bill Thomas and Jim Copeland group 12. We were all accommodated at the Selangor Bulk Oil Installation, about 6 miles from Kuala Selangor, and all trainees were accommodated in the same location. We still had to train and visit all the estates in the three groups and frequently at night and in the early hours of the morning check on the alertness or otherwise of guards on duty. One late afternoon five of us were out visiting estates in the district, leaving Jock Keen in charge of the training school. At about 6 p.m. the Malay corporal in charge of the guard reported to Jock Keen that a jungle pig was in the rubber plantation across the road. Jock picked up a Mark V .303 rifle (at the end of the war called the commando rifle): short, with rubber butt and flash eliminator. Jock's usual weapon was the sten gun. Jock and the corporal got to within 10 yards of the jungle pig. Jock fired a round and missed the pig, then fired a further four rounds all of which went astray. The pig quite naturally took off at speed. On our return to base the corporal told us what had happened, and didn't we give Jock a hard time?

Poor Jock was riled about this for at least a month, when it all happened again. Jock was on his own at the training camp when our Tamil cook came into the bungalow and told him that a jungle pig was on the other side of the bamboo hedge which separated our property from an Asian family next to us. This time Jock picked up his sten gun, inserted a full magazine (32 rounds, 9 mm ammunition) and stealthily made his way to the side of the bungalow. Sure enough, the pig was clearly visible through the bamboo hedge. Jock let go a fairly large burst of ammo and the pig was well and truly killed. The cook and his assistant dragged the pig through the bamboo hedge and laid it out on a concrete slab at the rear of the bungalow. They then boiled up water to scald the pig and scrub off the bristles. It was at this time that we returned and congratulated a delighted Jock Keen. While we were watching the scalding and scrubbing operations going on, an elderly Chinese lady who lived on a small rubber holding across the road from us came to the rear of the bungalow. She observed the frenzied work going on and after a short while said, in Malay, 'Itu saya poonya babi' (That is my pig). Poor Jock had killed a straying domestic pig.

From 1st January 1950 until the 14th May 1950 I was employed in the office of the officer in charge of the police district doing general police and administration duties. During this period I was also involved in numerous screening operations throughout the district. On 27th January Tim Hatton was transferred to Kuala Lumpur as personal assistant to the commissioner of police. The new officer in charge of the police district, Gerry Gill, arrived from Mentakab, Pahang on the afternoon of the same day. At 9 p.m. on 13th March I was called out to a murder incident on Rosevale estate where two Tamil special constables had murdered five Tamil coolies and wounded another two. They were arrested and charged with murder. At 3.15 p.m. on 5th April I was interviewed by Mr Cole, Superintendent of Police – officer in charge of the Klang Police Circle, which included the police districts of Kuala Selangor, Kajang and Klang. He told me that he was considering putting me forward for promotion to the gazetted (officer) rank but first of all I had to prove myself by:

(1) Doing one month's administration work (already completed);
(2) Investigating and solving three crimes; and
(3) Operating for 3 months with jungle squads.

On 9th April 1950 sergeants Seymour, Thomas, Keen, Copeland and myself went to Kuala Lumpur to have farewell drinks and a meal with Sergeant MacLean, who was leaving the force on compassionate grounds. We ended up the evening in the Eastern dance hall. As it was Easter weekend there was an extension until 1 a.m., at which time the only people left were the six of us at one table, a Scots Guard sergeant (known to us), sitting at a table on his own, the Philippino band, still playing, and the Chinese waiters. Two females, wives of the band, were the only couple on the floor. At this point the Scots Guard sergeant moved on to the floor, separated the two women and forced one to dance with him. The husband of the woman the sergeant had grabbed came down from the platform and hit the sergeant with a steel drum stick. The sergeant clouted the Philippino, knocking him out cold, and then took off. All the Philippino band members and all the Chinese waiters converged on our table.

We told Sergeant MacLean to get out fast, then the battle commenced. Tables, chairs, bottles and glasses were all used. We had to make a fighting retreat to the exit and during the retreat we were fairly well battered about the head. On getting to the door, Sergeant Seymour jumped into a trishaw and told the driver to take him to Campbell Road police station where he informed the police about the battle going on in the Eastern dance hall. The riot squad arrived and put an end to the fight. We were then all taken to the outpatients' department of the government hospital where our wounds were tended. From there we went to the CID office to be interrogated. At about 3 a.m. we were ushered into a large room with low lighting and a large desk in the far corner. A Malay was seated behind the desk. As we entered, he said, 'What have my boys been up to, now?' He turned out to be our former officer in charge of the police district at Kuala Selangor, Mohamed Ariffin. After taking brief statements he told us that we had obviously come off better in the battle because seven Chinese had been admitted to hospital. The outcome was that the Eastern dance hall was put out of bounds to the military.

Sleuth at work

On 12th April 1950 I was given my first case to investigate: the theft of 100 coconuts from Ujong Permatang estate of the Kuala Selangor group of estates. Two days later I arrested the thief, a Chinese male, who appeared at the magistrates' court, Kuala Selangor on 9th May, and was given a fine of 100 Malayan dollars or 3 weeks' rigorous imprisonment (hard labour). The fine was paid.

On the same day, 14th April, I was ordered by the officer in charge of the police district to investigate the theft of a lady's wrist watch from Dr P. West's bungalow, Bukit Rotan. Dr West and his wife Baie, a French national, had been to Singapore on 10 days' holiday and on their return to Bukit Rotan discovered the watch missing. I took a statement from Dr West as to the description, value and details of insurance. Dr West had bought the watch when released from Changi Internment camp in October 1945. Inscribed on the back of the watch were the following details: 'From Paddy to Baie, October 1945'. The watch was valued at 150 Malayan dollars and insured for £50.00. The doctor stated that the watch was of great sentimental value.

After taking statements from Mrs West and the three Chinese servants I was about to leave when Mrs West said that she was very grateful to me for coming along so soon to investigate the theft and with a very embarrassing slip of the tongue, I said, 'You are not half grateful enough.' What I had meant to say was that I hoped to make her more grateful. I embarrassedly tried to explain this but the damage had been done. As a result of that blunder I was determined to get the watch back. I was assured by Dr West and his wife that his servants were above suspicion – servants he had had for a number of years before the Japanese occupation. The only other people who could have had access to the bungalow were the corporal and three special constables assigned to guard the doctor's bungalow and dispensary. The corporal spoke good English, had been an outstanding NCO up to that time and was thoroughly trusted by me. I spoke to him at length about the theft but he was unable to throw any light on the matter and was also unable to say whether he suspected any of his men. I therefore had to interview all three.

The first two special constables showed no emotions, were

67

not fidgety, answered questions clearly and concisely and appeared to be in the clear. The third was a very different character. He kept shifting about, putting his hands in and out of his pockets, and generally looked liked a true suspect. I told him that I suspected him of the theft and would give him 2 minutes to get the watch and put it back on Dr West's dispensary table in the next room. He put his hand in his left pocket and pulled out a pawn ticket which he handed to me. I asked him what the pawn ticket was all about and he then said that he had stolen the watch and pawned it in the only pawn shop in Kuala Selangor. I then arrested the special constable, took him to the pawn shop in Kuala Selangor and recovered the watch. He had attempted to erase the inscription from the back of the watch. He was then charged before the local magistrate and was released on bail. He appeared in the magistrates' court, Kuala Selangor on the 8th May 1950 and was sentenced to 4 months' rigorous imprisonment. When Dr West was in the witness box identifying the watch, he spoke about the great sentimental value of the watch and made glowing remarks about the prompt and efficient investigation. This appeared in the local press, read by Superintendent Cole. He later telephoned the officer in charge of the police district and excused me the third investigation.

At 9 p.m. on 15th April 1950, terrorists walked into a shop in the village of Sekinchang, 20 miles to the north of Kuala Selangor, and shot dead the owner of the shop and his son for not supplying them with food and money. A special constable was also shot dead and a Chinese male wounded. As a result of this incident the village of Sekinchang was surrounded by police in the early hours of 23rd April and the 800 residents screened. Fourteen people were arrested, ten under the emergency regulations and four for national registration card offences.

Sekinchang village consisted of a fairly large fishing village with all houses constructed of bamboo walls and attap roofs.

All were built on stilts over a mangrove swamp, which meant that the high tides flowed and ebbed under the houses. All houses were connected with wooden walkways, again supported on stilts. Behind the Sekinchang village the government had opened up a large scheme of over 5000 acres to grow rice. To accomplish this they had blocked off the Sungei Tinggi (high river) and excavated a large irrigation ditch about 2 miles long, 14 feet deep and 70 yards wide. Off the main irrigation ditch smaller irrigation canals were excavated to irrigate the numerous allocated holdings to the mainly Chinese farmers in the area. So that the area would be properly policed, I was sent to Sekinchang with three jungle squads – 30 men in all (28 Malays and two Chinese).

We arrived in Sekinchang at 2 p.m. on 14th May and took over three water development huts about half a mile from the village. After getting the men settled in and organising guard duties, etc., I set off at 6.30 p.m. (dusk) to get a meal in the village. The Malay and Chinese rank and file had their own cooking arrangements but I had nothing to cook on and no suitable food. So off I went to eat in a Chinese coffee shop in the village. When about a quarter of a mile from the village I noted two shadowy figures following me at a distance. I did not give it a further thought and entered the first coffee shop I came across. I was armed with a sten gun. After having a meal of nasi goreng (fried rice), a favourite dish of mine, and a coffee I left the coffee shop. Seated outside the front door with a sten gun was one of my Chinese constables. The other Chinese constable was at the rear door. These two were the shadowy figures I had noticed earlier. This became regular practice for these two constables whenever I went anywhere on my own.

The inhabitants of the fishing village and in the large rice-growing area were almost entirely Chinese and were not at that time very cooperative; they were in fact anti-police. The coffee shop where I had all my meals was only some 50 yards from the shop where the murders and attempted murder had been committed by the terrorists.

I was stationed at Sekinchang from 14th May until 29th July 1950. During this period the three jungle squads under my command carried out continual patrols and ambushes, day and night, all over this large rice-growing area. Apart from a few arrests, mainly concerning identity card offences, possession of Communist Party documents and illegal possession of paddy (unhusked rice), nothing startling occurred and no contact was ever made with terrorists. During my stay in Sekinchang I had two visits from detachments of Royal Marines. The first detachment arrived on 11th June, being ferried ashore, by police launch towing a whaler, from the minesweeper *Jasseur*. This detachment of marines was off the cruiser *Kenya*, visiting Singapore. During their brief stay they were taken on patrol all over Sekinchang and Tanjong Karang areas. Some of the patrols were cycle patrols which was fine if the weather was dry. If wet, the mud was a real sticky mess which clogged up the wheels; and on many an occasion it was impossible to push the cycle and there was nothing for it but to carry the cycle on one's shoulder. During the visit of the first detachment of marines I made the following entry in my diary:

15.6.50: very heavy rain – unable to patrol – area a sea of mud.

When conditions were as bad as that, one contented oneself by remembering that the enemy (terrorists) were also being hampered. Another detachment of marines arrived on the day the first detachment left, 20th June. They came ashore from the frigate *Morecambe Bay*, and were from the cruiser *Mauritius*. They were recalled on the 24th June 1950.

On my arrival in Sekinchang the Sekinchang police station was a wooden building on stilts situated over a mangrove swamp. The only way one could approach the station was by a wooden bridge over a deep monsoon ditch. All around the station was otherwise impassable swampy ground. The station staff consisted of a sergeant and six constables. A new police station – a solid brick and mortar building – was under construction at the time, at the rear of Sekinchang village. This was occupied for the first time on 24th June 1950 when I and two jungle squads moved into the station.

At the same time on the jungle fringe at the rear of the large rice-growing area, a two-storey water development building known as the Headworks was taken over and turned into a police station. This station was named Sawah Sempadam police station. It was officially opened on 1st June 1950 and on most days from that date until 27th July 1950 a section of men and I travelled from Sekinchang to erect defences around the station. The entire defence system, including bunkers, was erected by my men. Local materials were used except for barbed wire and staples. Sandbag defence posts were of no use in Malaya. In the humid atmosphere sacks rotted in a matter of weeks. Defence bunkers were constructed as follows: a row of poles about 24 inches apart were driven into the ground in the shape of a square. An outer row was then driven into the ground in a similar fashion, leaving a gap of from 18 to 24 inches between the outer and inner rows. Boards or poles were then fixed horizontally to the upright poles and the middle was then filled in with whatever type of soil was available. Over the top of the defence bunker an attap roof was constructed to protect one from the elements, i.e., torrential rain and heat.

Crocodile

At 10 a.m. on the morning of 28th June 1950, while we were working on the defences at the police station, a local Malay came rushing up to the police station on his bicycle and reported that a crocodile responsible for the deaths of three women was sunning itself on the far side of the main irrigation canal. Over a period of time the women had been snatched

71

when washing clothes down the canal bank. I picked up a Lee Enfield .303 rifle and jumped on the carrier of the bicycle, telling the Malay to take me to the spot. We travelled about 500 yards along the path below the bund wall of the irrigation canal. The Malay stopped and we both quietly crawled up the bund wall to have a look at the crocodile. The crocodile had given up sunning himself on the far side of the canal and was moving up the canal towards us. All I could see was the head and occasionally a glimpse of part of the crocodile's back.

I estimated the crocodile to be about 90 yards distant. Being afraid that the creature would spot us and submerge, I took aim behind the right eye and fired one shot. There was a lot of thrashing about and the crocodile disappeared. In no time a large crowd of Malays and a few Chinese gathered. Someone went for a sampan (Malay boat) and, armed with a long pole to which a three prong barb was attached (and attached to the barb a long length of rope) they pushed off into the canal. They prodded around for a long time and suddenly there was great excitement. They had located the crocodile but could not get the barb to pierce the skin. At about 2 p.m. they had success, the barb entering the soft part of the crocodile's tail. They pulled the crocodile to the surface and over to the bank. By this time about 100 people had assembled and were struggling to get the crocodile up the bank; they were making little progress.

A Chinese foreman from the water development department happened to come along and view the situation. He suggested that they cut stout poles from trees in the jungle, 6 to 8 feet long, and that about eight such poles might be worked under the crocodile's body; then, with eight men either side, the crocodile could be carried bodily up the bank. This worked. I had a jeep with me that day and the crocodile was carried on to the jeep. The head of the crocodile was hanging over the radiator, windscreen folded down, and the tail was on the road at the rear of the jeep. The driver and I set off for the nearest tarmac road, which was 7 miles away, leading to the nearest town, Tanjong Karang. During the journey over the rough track three springs were broken.

The crocodile was 15 feet 3 inches long and weighed over half a ton. When we reached Tanjong Karang the crocodile was winched on to a 15 cwt Chevrolet truck and taken to Kuala Lumpur, where it was paraded up and down Batu Road, the main street. By coincidence it was a public holiday in Malaya called Hari Raya Haji to celebrate the return of pilgrims from Mecca. Following the publicity my sergeant friend at the Selangor Bulk Oil Installation, Roy Warrington Seymour, composed the following poem:

The Passing of the Terror of Tanjong Karang

Come gather round my children, draw closer to my side,
While I tell you the tale of a killer, and how that killer died;
'Twas a friend of mine that shot him, I well remember the day
When the Terror of Tanjong Karang on a jeep was carried away.

It happened in the evening, when the word was passed around
That just up by the Headworks the killer could be found;
Now Mathieson was at that place, he's my friend you see,
And he hastened to the rendezvous with his trusty .303.

The killer saw him coming and tried to break and run,
But Mathieson was quicker and a bullet left his gun;
Only one shot was fired, he didn't need fire again,
For that bullet from his rifle had found the killer's brain.

So the people walk the beaches and remember with a smile
When Mathieson, with one shot, slayed the killer crocodile.
There's a moral to the story; it's plain for all to see –
No matter how fast you can run you can't beat a .303.

R. W. Seymour 1.7.50.

I was offered a reward by the district commissioner of Kuala Selangor for killing the man-eating crocodile. This was officially laid down at 3 cents an inch, a total of 5 dollars 49 cents (13 shillings and sixpence at the then British exchange rates – about 70 pence now). I told the district commissioner to keep the money.

On the 15th June 1950 I was called to the office of the officer in charge of the police district, Kuala Selangor for an interview. I was told that I was one of the sergeants selected to go before a selection board in Kuala Lumpur with the possibility of being promoted to the commissioned rank (known in Malaya as gazetted rank). At 10 a.m. on 16th June I was interviewed by the officer superintending the police circle, Klang – Superintendent Cole – and at 2.30 p.m. on the same day I was interviewed by the deputy chief police officer, Selangor State. From 8 a.m. to 1.40 p.m. on 17th June I waited at the labour office, Kuala Lumpur, for an interview with the selection board. The members of the board comprised the director of labour, the director of establishments and the deputy commissioner of police, Mr Urquhart. I was unable to get an interview owing to the large number of candidates present, 66 men, and was told to report again at 9 a.m. on the 21st June. I did this and during the interview the deputy commissioner of police asked about my education. I told him that full details of my education were in the file in front of him and explained that my education could possibly have been much better had my parents had the funds to put me on for further education but instead I had had to leave school when I was just 14 years old. I was aware that, pre-war, only candidates with university degrees had been admitted into the Malayan police service, so I thought I may as well get my say in first.

Surprisingly, Mr Urquhart said, 'Mathieson, you are right – that was the case in the past – but it no longer applies.' He went on to say that they had discovered good or even better material as officers for the force who had never seen the inside of a university. He added, 'Don't let your education worry you.' The questions from the other members of the board were fairly routine and I was dismissed and told that I would be informed of the result of the interview shortly.

Good news – but a precious memento is confiscated

On 9th July 1950 I received a telephone call from Gerry Gill, OCPD, Kuala Selangor, congratulating me on my promotion to the gazetted rank, which was subject to my passing a medical examination. On 10th July I attended Bungsar Hospital, Kuala Lumpur, for a medical and x-rays and got a clean bill of health. Of the 66 candidates put forward at the selection board only three were successful.

On 15th July 1950 I was officially notified by the commissioner of police of my promotion. The local people at Sekinchang had in the meantime heard of my promotion and my impending transfer out of the area. On the morning of 28th July 1950 I was approached by the headmaster of the Chinese school who could speak good English. He told me that I had been invited to a dinner by the headmen of Sekinchang that night and asked for my initials and the proper spelling of my name. I thought this rather strange but gave him the details. The dinner was held in a coffee shop in the village and was attended by 16 male Chinese. Seated at the head of the table, or bottom, was the senior headman, well over 80 years of age. I was seated at the bottom of the table, or top, and seated beside me was the Chinese headmaster.

After an excellent Chinese dinner the senior headman got up and spoke at length. The schoolmaster sitting beside me interpreted what he said. The general theme of his speech was that prior to our arrival they had been suspicious of the police and were in fact anti-police. This had all changed because of the fair treatment they had received from all my men and because we had carried out our duties in a professional and friendly way. He particularly referred to the fact

75

that I frequently stopped and talked to the children and patted them on the head. Congratulating me on my promotion and regretting that I was leaving the area he asked me to accept as a token of their appreciation a small gift to remind me of my days in Sekinchang. The gift was then handed over by the schoolmaster which was a gold Shaeffer pen and pencil set in a presentation box with my name, W. P. Mathieson, engraved on pen and pencil. I thanked the senior headman for his kind words and said that I had thoroughly enjoyed my stay in Sekinchang amongst friends. I referred particularly to the coffee shop where I had all my delightful meals and where I was treated as one of their own.

At 3 p.m. on the 29th July 1950 I left Sekinchang for Kuala Selangor on transfer to Johore State. On arriving in Kuala Selangor I told Gerry Gill, officer in charge of the police district, about my dinner and presentation from the elders of Sekinchang village. Gerry said that I had accepted a bribe and would have to hand it over. I remonstrated with him, saying that it was a goodwill gesture by the people of Sekinchang and that if I had refused to attend the dinner or accept the gift it would have been a slap in the face to people who we were desperately trying to win over to the government side. Gerry did agree that it would have been wrong to refuse to accept the gift or attend the dinner, and as I was being transferred 300 miles away it was very doubtful to say the least whether anyone from Sekinchang or elsewhere would term the gift a bribe; nevertheless, he had to refer the matter to higher authority. That was the last I heard of it. I never saw the gold Shaeffer pen and pencil set again but was told unofficially that all such gifts were sold and proceeds went to the general revenue. Why anyone would want to buy something with my name on it I don't know. I felt very bitter about it at the time and still do.

At 2 p.m. on 31st July I left Kuala Selangor for Kuala Lumpur and at 8 p.m. that night left on the night train for Johore. At 7.15 a.m. on the 1st August I arrived at Johore

Bahru railway station and at 10 a.m. was interviewed by Paddy Jackson, Chief Police Officer, Johore State who told me that I was being posted to the Kota Tinggi Police Circle. I left at midday for Kota Tinggi, arriving at 1 p.m. I was interviewed by the officer superintending the police circle, Charles Greenstreet. He told me that I was being appointed to the post of administration officer for the police circle which covered the three police districts of Mersing, Kota Tinggi and Pengerang. The administration job consisted of routine administration such as transfers, leave, promotions, ordering of rations and stores, etc; I was also asked by the OSPC to put everyone in Kota Tinggi police district through a course of firing on the range. On 6th August 1950 I was in my office when in walked Commissioner of Police W. N. Gray CMG DSO, with my boss, Supt Charles Greenstreet. After I'd been introduced to the commissioner he asked what my job was. I told him that I was administrative officer for the Kota Tinggi Police Circle.

'How long,' he asked, 'have you been in Kota Tinggi?'

Five days,' I replied.

'Have you been around the police circle?'

'No sir.'

'How the hell can you administer something when you don't know what you are administering?' He turned to Superintendent Greenstreet and said, 'Get him out.'

Apart from the three district police headquarters at Mersing, Kota Tinggi and Pengerang, each district had about six outstations and that was my first task – to visit all these stations and get to know the area and problems for myself. From 1st August 1950 until 25th October 1950 I carried out my duties as administrative officer; during this time I visited 18 police stations and numerous estates by road and river. The road to Mersing was classified a red road (where frequent ambushes took place) and one had to travel either in an armoured personnel carrier or in a two or more vehicle convoy. During the same period I put 200 regular police from the Kota Tinggi police district through a firing course on the range.

A Tough Job – And Another Tough Year

On 20th October 1950 I was told by Charles Greenstreet that Tom Lilley, the officer in charge of the Kota Tinggi police district, was resigning; I was asked to take over his post by 25th October. This was a heavy responsibility in that I was suddenly in overall command of 200 regular rank and file police officers, 500 special constables guarding rubber estates and tin mines and 2500 auxiliary police and home guards who were recruited to guard new villages, kampongs (Malay villages), etc.

At 7 a.m. on the morning of 25th November 1950 I accompanied a jungle squad which was called to a small Chinese-owned rubber holding 1½ miles from Kota Tinggi. On the previous evening, a gang of terrorists had called at the small holding belonging to an elderly Chinese male, whose only daughter lived with him, taking food and everything of value. They shot the elderly male through the right eye and cut off one of his fingers to get a gold ring. The old man was taken to the hospital for a post-mortem examination because the bullet had failed to exit through the skull. It turned out that the ammunition used was very old and although the victim had been shot at close range – there were powder burns around his eye – the bullet failed to go through the skull. This was the first of many post-mortems I had to attend and it was not a pleasant one. The doctor cut off the top of the skull with a small electric saw and retrieved the spent bullet from the old man's brain.

On returning to the station I was told that a launch on its way down the Kambau River had been fired upon by terrorists and that a special constable had been killed and a police corporal wounded. I left for Kambau with two jungle squads, travelling in two unprotected launches. At 1.30 p.m. we arrived at the ambush position, drove both launches into the river bank and jumped ashore. The terrorists had fled. An inspection of the ambush area revealed ambush positions for about 15 people, each ambush position being in touch with the next. Jungle creepers had been tied together for some form of warning. From 7 p.m. to 6 a.m. on 26th November we laid ambushes on tracks to and from the Kambau estate rubber tappers' accommodation but nothing occurred. At 10 a.m. we left Kambau for Kuala Sedili and at 1 p.m. attended the funeral of the special constable. We returned to Kota Tinggi at 7.30 p.m.

At 2 p.m. on 27th November I accompanied the administrative officer, George Patterson, and the commanding officer of the 2nd/2nd Gurkha Rifles to the 3rd milestone on the Mawai Road after a report of a shoot-up between Gurkhas and terrorists. The incident took place near Kampong Lukut. One Gurkha other rank was killed. The Gurkhas recovered two Lee Enfield rifles from wounded terrorists who escaped.

At 9.10 p.m. on Friday 20th December I received a call from the desk officer at the police station that I was required there immediately. I arrived at the station at 9.15 p.m. and came upon a male Chinese being interviewed by the station sergeant. He turned out to be a headman from the Sisek Tin Mines and was reporting an ambush on the railway line about a mile from the mine. The details he had were scant but were to the effect that a number of police and labourers from the mine had been killed or wounded when ambushed by terrorists. The police were escorting food and other supplies to the mine. I informed my boss, Charles Greenstreet. He in turn notified Lt. Col. Cruikshanks, commanding officer of the 2nd/2nd Gurkha Rifles. Within 10 minutes we all met in the operations room at the Kota Tinggi police station; included at the meeting were the military and police operations officers.

The commanding officer of the Gurkhas stated that he could not supply any troops until daylight and would then mount an extended operation. I stated to my boss that it was wrong to leave the wounded until the following morning and that I intended to leave immediately provided that I could

79

rustle together a section of men. This he immediately agreed to. It turned out that all jungle squads were on operations away from the station. I eventually got together eight constables, bar officers from the police station and court officers who worked at the magistrates' court. A new British police officer had been posted to Kota Tinggi district that day. He was Dan Woods, assistant superintendent of police, an ex-lieutenant from the Royal Navy. Dan volunteered to come along.

At 10.50 p.m. we embarked on a hired launch just in front of the police station and headed up the river to the landing stage for Sisek Tin Mines. This was in the middle of the monsoon season so there was torrential rain and it was very dark. There was no place to shelter in the launch and we were naturally saturated in a short time. At midnight we arrived at the landing stage. Sisek Tin Mines were six miles away along a narrow gauge railway track. On landing, I sorted out the section: two constables in front, leading scouts, I was third man followed by the other six constables, with Dan Woods taking up the rear. We then discovered that it was so dark that it was impossible to keep in touch without some sort of aid. Torches were out of the question. We decided to take our lanyards off, tie them all together and hold on to this with the left hand. We then set off at a very slow pace walking on slimy green sleepers in the centre of the track.

There were numerous streams running under the railway line and quite a number of mishaps occurred, with men slipping off sleepers and falling into the streams. During one of these incidents the bren gunner lost two magazines; this was the subject of an enquiry later. Before we had left Kota Tinggi police station the Gurkha operations officer had handed over a small tin of rum to Dan Woods and myself. The Gurkhas were issued with a rum ration in those days and the rum was tinned to enable rations to be dropped from the air. After travelling for what we thought to be an hour we sampled the rum, which was quite good. It was so dark even then that it was impossible to identify who was sitting next to you. The canopy of trees above us was over 100 feet high and it continued to rain.

We kept plodding on and at 5 a.m. on rounding a bend in the railway track the two constables immediately in front of me stopped and whispered 'penjahat' (terrorists). About 100 yards ahead there was a fire burning and they assumed that the terrorists had camped for the night. I went back along the line and informed the section what was ahead. I took the bren gun from the bren gunner and gave him my .300 carbine. I then took the lead, moving off the track and keeping as close as possible to the jungle fringe on the right of the track. The fire appeared to be on the left of the track although this was difficult to determine with the curve in the track. We moved cautiously forward and when I was about 50 yards from the fire something white loomed up in front of me. This turned out to be the body of a Chinese male stripped of his clothing.

As we progressed step by step other bodies appeared, and when we arrived where the fire was burning we discovered that the terrorists had set the locomotive on fire and that the engine oil was still burning. The terrorists had vanished. It had taken us 5 hours to travel 5 miles and we still had a mile to go to the mine. We carried on and as daylight was breaking at about 6.15 a.m. we hailed the police on duty at the mine and identified ourselves. We then learned that the ambush had taken place at about 4 p.m. and the shooting had been heard from the mine. A section of constables from the mine went to investigate and had a brief shoot-out with the terrorists who then made off. The section of constables then removed all the wounded back to the mine where they were given first aid. We always carried sulphonamide powder and bandages with us and we again treated the wounded. It turned out that five special constables had been killed and the sixth received five bullet wounds. Two Chinese workers from the mine had also been killed and five wounded. The terrorists had got away with six rifles and 300 rounds of ammunition, plus food and stores. The gang of terrorists from the ambush positions laid were estimated to be 30/40 strong.

After resting for an hour all the wounded were placed on flat trollies. On our way back down the track we loaded on the seven dead (five constables and two Chinese workmen) and pushed the trollies all the way down to the river. What amazed me was the fact that after only 16 hours small white maggots were crawling on the dead bodies. We arrived back at the river at midday, 21st December, and loaded the wounded and dead on to the waiting launch. When travelling down river I had an itchy feeling on my legs and on checking discovered that I had a total of 23 leeches clinging to me. They were lovely and fat – full of blood. The only thing which removes leeches without causing ulcers is to put salt on them or burn them off with a cigarette end. As I had no salt, the latter sufficed. In my rush to go to the police station the previous evening I had pulled on a pair of ankle baseball boots which are of no use in leech country. I should have dressed in jungle boots which are knee length canvas boots with rubber soles which lace right up to the knee with the trouser legs tucked inside. Later when looking at a map of the area I was pleasantly surprised to read that one of the jungle hills we had passed near the railway track was Bukit Patchett (Leech Hill). At 1.30 p.m. we arrived back at Kota Tinggi police station where the wounded were immediately taken to the Kota Tinggi and Johore Bahru hospitals. From 1.30 p.m. to 5.10 p.m. I had to attend post-mortems on the dead. I am glad to say that all the wounded recovered.

On the 16th January 1951 I went on 6 days' leave to Johore Bahru to study for a Malay language examination due on the 22nd and 23rd of the month. I was called back to Kota Tinggi on the 18th January because of floods. The Kota Tinggi district police headquarters was situated on the bank of the Kota Tinggi river and after torrential rain for 14 days and nights the river had risen 21 feet. The water of the river was normally 15 feet below the ground level of the police station.

When I arrived back on the morning of the 18th the police station was flooded to a depth of 6 feet. It was fortunate that the station was a two-storey building with the main offices on the upper floor. Everyone had to evacuate the station including all the prisoners in the cells and all police and families who lived in married quarters behind the building. A temporary station was set up on higher ground near the magistrates' court. The flooding didn't recede until 24th January and the only way one could get around was by one military-supplied DUKW (amphibious landing craft) and a number of commando-type canvas boats, also supplied by the military.

The mainly-Chinese population of Kota Tinggi continued to live in the upper stories of their houses and were supplied with food organised by rationing officers under the command of the administration officer for Kota Tinggi, Mr George Patterson. The battalion of the 2nd/2nd Gurkha Rifles, billeted on the outskirts of the town, had their supplies dropped to them by Dakota aircraft. Bundles of rations were dropped by parachute at or near to the Gurkhas' camp. The young Chinese boys used to climb on to the roofs of their houses from the open verandah on the front of the upper storey to watch the Dakota coming in to drop the supplies.

On one particular day one of the young Chinese boys slipped off the roof and on his way down into the flooded street below grabbed the high tension cables running along the front of the buildings. Fortunately for this young boy, at almost exactly the same time, the parachute attached to a bundle of rations failed to open and the bundle of rations struck the high tension cables about half a mile away, thereby cutting off the power. The boy fell into the water and was immediately picked up by a police patrol in one of the canvas boats. Apart from having one hand scorched, he was in perfect health.

On Saturday 27th January 1951 a report was received that rubber trees had been slashed on Kambau rubber estate and that a headman was missing from the nearby Gemriah estate.

From 11.45 a.m. to 1.05 p.m. I flew over Kambau estate and Kambau police station in an Auster aircraft but could see no sign of terrorists. At 8.30 a.m. on Sunday 28th I left Kota Tinggi with Police Lieutenant Bill Berry and two jungle squads for Kambau. On the way we visited the Mawai Settlement and Mawai police station. At 10 a.m. we left Mawai by launch and proceeded to Gemriah estate. From 11.30 a.m. to 3 p.m. we searched for the missing headman without success. At 3 p.m. we left Gemriah estate, arriving at Kambau estate at 4.30 p.m. where I inspected the slashed area of rubber. We left Kambau at 6.30 p.m. and arrived at Kuala Sedili 2 hours later. At 10.30 a.m. on the 29th we returned to Gemriah estate to make further enquiries; there was still no trace of the missing headman. We returned to Kota Tinggi at 2.30 p.m.

On 5th February 1951 I received a report from the Kuala Sedili police that terrorists were reported to be in an area north of Kuala Sedili. I left Kota Tinggi at 10.30 p.m. with one jungle squad. We arrived at Kuala Sedili police station at 3.30 a.m. on 6th February. At 5.30 a.m. we commenced operating in the Kampong Semanchang area north of Kuala Sedili with one jungle squad and a section of auxiliary police. We came upon a small camp for four people which had recently been evacuated. At 10 p.m. on the same day in the Kampong Seman-chang area we arrested four Chinese males, all carrying mili-tary-type terrorist packs but no arms. At 9.30 a.m. on the 8th February we left Kuala Sedili with the four prisoners; we arrived at Kota Tinggi at 2 p.m. The prisoners were handed over to the special branch for interrogation. Documents found in the packs were also handed over for translation.

At about this time I was approached by a business col-league of Mr Tan Chen Lock, a Singapore Chinese business-man and member of the Singapore Legislative Council. Mr Tan owned the 8000-acre Kambau rubber estate, which was in a very isolated area and could only be reached by a narrow winding river with banks on both sides covered with dense tropical forest. I was offered the post of security officer on the estate at a salary of 1400 Malayan dollars a month (approximately £164.00) plus free food and accommodation. This was a very tempting offer at a time when I, as officer in charge of the police district, was being paid 500 Malayan dollars a month with no food. I declined the offer.

The Kambau rubber estate was protected by a police force of 30 men under the command of a Malayan police corporal who was the officer in charge of the station OCS. Until that time there had been a number of terrorist attacks directed at the police and the estate; these mainly consisted of such incidents as terrorists shooting up unarmoured launches carrying police personnel to and from the estate and the slashing of rubber trees. The most serious incident occurred on 28th June 1950 when an estimated 100 terrorists attacked the police station, killing two constables and wounding three others. Seven terrorists were believed to have been killed or wounded. During the engagement the terrorists shot away the radio aerial, thereby cutting off the only means of contact with police headquarters in Kota Tinggi. The radio operator, a police constable, went outside the police station, rigged up a temporary aerial and got back in touch with police headquarters at Kota Tinggi, who sent up reinforcements. This constable was awarded the colonial police medal for gallantry.

Mr Tan later recruited one of my men, Police Lieutenant Williamson, an ex-Royal Marine. He took over the post of security officer of Kambau estate after resigning from the force. He was appointed an honorary police inspector. A short time later, while accompanying a section of police from the estate, he shot and killed two terrorists. For this he was awarded the colonial police medal for meritorious service. Not many months later, he himself was ambushed and killed on Kambau estate. At around the same time another of my police lieutenants, Bill Berry, resigned from the force and took up an appointment as security officer on a Lee Pineapple Plantation in another district in Johore. At 6 a.m. one morning, when opening up the compound gate to search workers going

out to work, he was shot down and killed by communist terrorists waiting for him. Bill Berry was a very fine officer who had
accompanied me on a number of patrols and ambushes in
the Kambau and Kuala Sedili areas.

On the morning of 23 February 1951 I was with one jungle
squad when we laid an ambush from 4.35 a.m. to 9 a.m. in
the Pelepah Valley rubber estate. We had received information
from rubber tappers that terrorists used a particular path and
were due to collect food that morning. Nothing occurred. On
returning to Kota Tinggi police station I was informed that
the police station and quarters being built for the special
constabulary at Susor Rotan Tin Mines had been burnt down
by terrorists on the previous evening. The special constables
had been due to take over the station on Saturday morning,
24th February. With one jungle squad I proceeded to Susor
Rotan which was situated in hilly jungle country 8 miles from
Lee Sawmill No. 2, on the nearest tarmac road.

The road to Susor Rotan was very rough, with dense
jungle on both sides and many hairpin bends. It was only
passable by four-wheel-drive vehicles. We left Kota Tinggi at
10.50 a.m. and arrived back at 4.30 p.m. Every incident had
to be investigated, this particular case being arson. The police
post at Susor Rotan was being opened up to prevent food,
money and medicines going to the terrorists in the area. The
only people living in Susor Rotan were Chinese tin miners
who worked four mines in the area. The district war executive
committee had for a time been considering closing down the
mines but the Chinese owners said that they would construct
the police station and quarters, erect defence posts and
enclose the area with a stout security fence at no cost to the
government. This had now all been undone. After returning
from Susor Rotan I was informed that there was a battle in
progress on Mawai estate, about 3 miles from the station. With
the same jungle squad, I sped to the estate and, following the
sound of gunshots, found that the battle was between special
constables from the estate who were on patrol near the jungle

fringe and a platoon of Gurkha Rifles who had emerged from the jungle. Fortunately, there were no casualties.

Almost since the state of emergency had been declared similar incidents to this had been a frequent occurrence because the police did not know in what areas the military were operating and the military did not know where the police were operating. It was laid down thereafter that all operations had to be cleared by the operations room at the district police headquarters to ensure that units were not operating in the same area. After the burning of the station and quarters I attended a district war executive committee meeting (24th February) when I proposed that the mines be closed down as it would be impossible to change over the police personnel at Susor Rotan without the serious risk of the loss of life during ambushes by terrorists anywhere along the terrible road from Lee Sawmill No. 2 to Susor Rotan. I also argued that the loss of the mines would not affect the economy of the country. The DWEC meeting was attended by the officer superintending the police circle, the commanding officer of the 2nd/2nd Gurkha Rifles, the circle special branch officer, the officer in charge of the police district (myself), the administrative officer who was also a senior magistrate, the district officer, two leading local officials and a representative from the tin miners. My appeal for the closure of the mines was turned down and the Chinese owners volunteered to rebuild the station and quarters.

On 5th March 1951 information was received that about ten terrorists would be coming in to pick up food from the Kampong Lukut area early in the morning of the 6th March. An ambush was laid by two jungle squads under the command of the police operations officer, C. J. Frazier, and two assistant superintendents of police, Dan Woods and D. R. Halford-Watkins. The exact track that the terrorists would use was not clear and when they appeared they were moving into the rear of the ambush position. The ambush party had to reverse their positions immediately and open fire. Four terrorists were shot dead; the remainder escaped.

From 11.45 a.m. to 6.45 p.m. on 9th March 1951 I accompanied one jungle squad to Lubok Pusing where we burnt down empty kongsis and confiscated two sampans (boats) on the river Sedili at Lubok Pusing estate. At 8.30 a.m. on the 10th March 1951 I left Kota Tinggi to visit Kambau police station and Kambau rubber estate. At midday I left Kambau and visited Gemriah estate where I met Penghulu Abdul Hadi, the penghulu (headman) of Mawai, and made arrangements with him to resettle the residents of Gemriah into one area; we also discussed the resettling of all shops in the Kuala Kambau area. I returned to Kota Tinggi at 5.15 p.m.

At 6.05 a.m. on 10th April I was called to the Kota Tinggi police station to be told that Kambau police station was under attack. The radio signal was distorted and the message unclear (morse). I got in touch with the military at Johore Bahru to arrange for the use of an Auster aircraft to fly over Kambau. At 6.45 a.m. the Auster, piloted by an army sergeant, landed on the football field behind the police station. We immediately took off and from 7.15 a.m. to 8.05 a.m. flew over Kambau rubber estate and Kambau police station. Everything appeared to be in order. At 10.50 a.m. on the same day I left Kota Tinggi with police lieutenant Berry and a jungle squad for Mawai and Kuala Sedili. We arrived at Kuala Sedili at 3.30 p.m. From 8.30 a.m. to 1 p.m. on the 11th April we carried out a patrol of Sedili Kechil and the Kampong Bahru area. At 2.30 p.m. we left Kuala Sedili for Kambau, arriving at 4.30 p.m. At 8.30 a.m. on the 12th April we left Kambau for Gemriah estate to meet penghulus Abdul Hadi, Osman and Tanah. We arranged the resettling of Gemriah and the posting of a permanent section of auxiliary police to guard the settled area. We returned to Kota Tinggi at 3.40 p.m.

At about 5 p.m. on 16th April 1951 information was received by telephone from Lee Sawmill No. 2, Lombong, that about 30 terrorists had stopped four logging trucks on their

St. Margarets Hope Higher Grade Public School 1938-39. Author No.15 back row.

Hunda Barrier construction workers 1940-41. Back row No.5 James Gow No.6 Peter Budge No.7 James Annal, all local men from South Ronaldsay. Standing extreme right construction boss Mr Bennett, seated next to him his son Ralph Bennett. The other workers came from Glasgow and southern Ireland.

Author number four from left.

Recruit training IIth Infantry Training Centre (Seaforth & Cameron) Pinefield Camp. Elgin, Morayshire, Scotland - September 1944.

Author dressed for quarter guard mounting Jakarta, Java, Indonesia December 1945. First time kilts had been worn in battalion since end of war.

After Indonesian extremists had been driven out of Bandoeng and from the Dutch market gardens at Lembang eight miles from Bandoeng in mid March 1946 I was sent with a section of men to guard the Lembang Observatory and surrounding area.

Author and wife with Bill Omand, Royal Military Police in background.

Wedding reception Venning Road Police Mess, Kuala Lumpur, Malaya 10 October 1953. Mrs Vera Lakin matron of honour author and wife.

Victoria Falls, Zambesi River near Livingstone, Zambia 21 June 1962.

Ministry of Defence Police CID conference Clyde Submarine Base, Faslane 1972. Seated extreme left author, Next to author Superintendent Pat Tierney, CID boss Northern Area.

Presentation of base plaque and citation by commanding officer United States Navy Base, Edzell, Angus, Scotland. Captain W.K. Martin, commanding officer, Detective Constable David Barnes, Legal Officer U.S. Navy and author.

Author - Officer in Charge of the Kota Tinggi Police District, Johore, Malaya 1950 - 51.

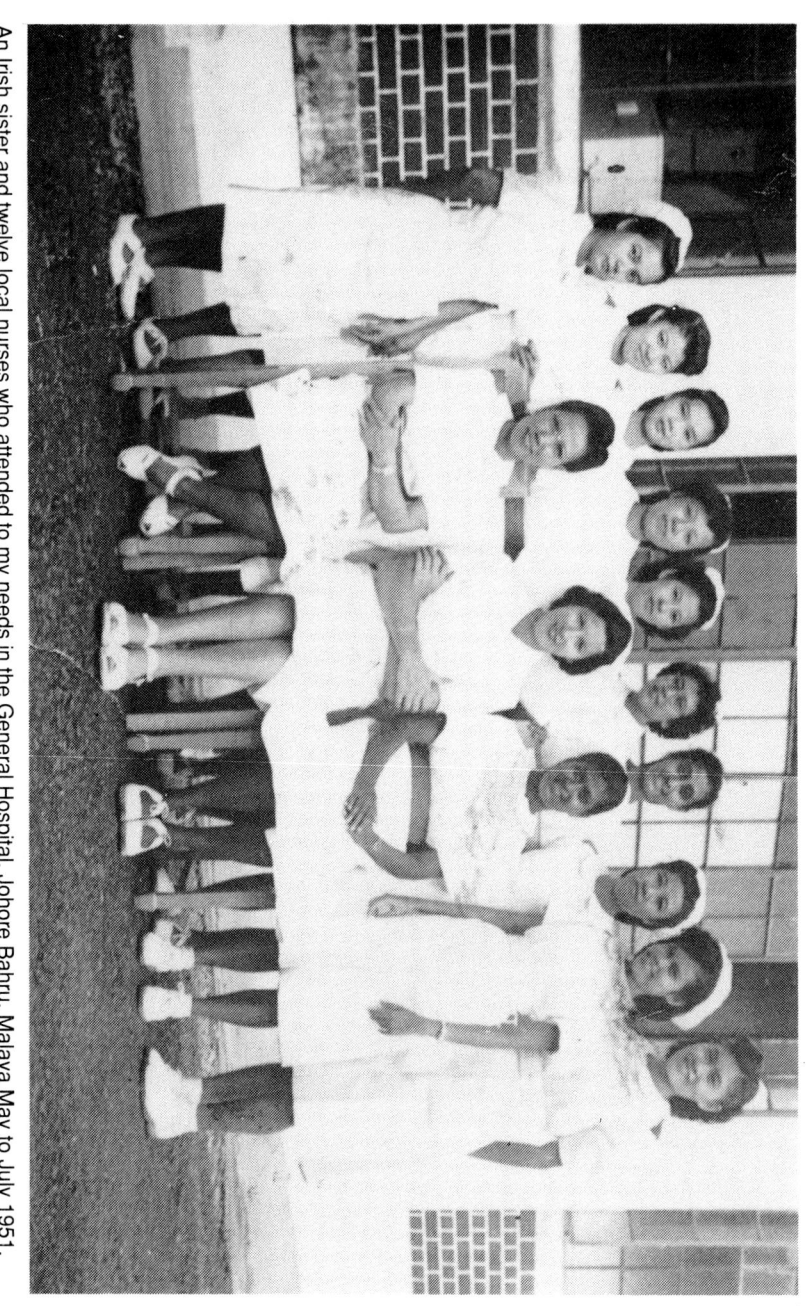

An Irish sister and twelve local nurses who attended to my needs in the General Hospital, Johore Bahru, Malaya May to July 1951.

Extreme left brother Police Lieutenant David Mathieson and other officers Federation of Malaya Police, Pahang State, Malaya 1951.

Jungle and Rubber Estate areas near Sungei Besi, Selangor State, Malaya where sonic tests were carried out for the Director of Operations, Kuala Lumpur. The author was in charge of the escort when all ground and air tests were carried out in 1953.

My platoon No.8 platoon 'C' company 1st battalion Seaforth Highlanders marching through the town of Kampar, Perak State, North Malaya November 1946.

Glugor Barracks, Penang Island, Malaya. Training of local enlisted personnel by 'C' company 1st Seaforths 1947.

Jungle Training School, Kuala Kubu Bahru, Selangor State, Malaya 1949. Back row No.2 Jock Keen No.6 Jim Copeland. Front row extreme left author.

Sekinchang, North Selangor, Malaya 1950. Left to right Sergeant Roy Seymour, Author, Sergeant Bill Thomas and Inspector Lim from CID headquarters, Kuala Lumpur.

Crocodile known locally as the terror of Tanjong Karang shot by author 28 June 1950 at Headworks behind Sekinchang Village, Kuala Selangor District.

way back to the sawmill at the end of work that day, relieved all the loggers of their identity cards (which were put in a heap and burnt), and then set the four logging trucks on fire. The incident had taken place about 4 miles from Lee Sawmill No. 2 on the road to the Susor Rotan Tin Mines. Cyril J. Frazier, the police operations officer, came to my office and said he would go out with jungle squads immediately to investigate the burning. I told him to leave it until the following morning because there were no reports of casualties and it would be dark in a matter of an hour. I also mentioned that when he did go out in the morning he should beware of a possible ambush and that any ambush might not be at the place where the trucks were burnt.

Two jungle squads under the command of the police operations officer and two assistant superintendents of police set off in the morning in Land-Rovers and one armoured personnel carrier. On their way they picked up the security officer from Lee Sawmill No. 2, Mr Sutherland, plus two special constables. Mr Sutherland was an ex-British police sergeant. They crawled along the logging road in four wheel drive and after travelling for 2 miles were ambushed. The security officer from the sawmill was in the leading Land-Rover and a shell was detonated under the Land-Rover which put it out of action. During the initial seconds of the ambush and the battle that ensued a policeman was killed and a further eight, including Mr Sutherland, were wounded.

At 11.30 a.m. news of the ambush was relayed to Kota Tinggi police station and I quickly accompanied Peter Rice (the officer superintending the police circle) and police and military to the area to evacuate the killed and wounded. On our arrival the terrorists had fled. We accounted for everyone with the exception of Mr Sutherland. After following spots of blood we came across him in a ravine close to a stream about a quarter of a mile from the road. He was immediately given a morphine injection, having a large wound in the hip. We had to construct a stretcher out of branches of trees and groundsheets and after a struggle got back to the road where he and the remainder of the wounded were transported to the Johore Bahru general hospital. Following this I had to take statements from all witnesses for the offences of murder, attempted murder, robbery and arson, the latter two offences in connection with the taking and burning of identity cards and the burning of the logging trucks.

At the next district war executive committee meeting I put my point forward again that this ambush had taken place on the Lee Sawmill No. 2–Susor Rotan road, and that it was now time to close down the Susor Rotan Tin Mines – the place where the terrorists were obviously being supplied with food, medicines, information, etc. The DWEC agreed to the closing down of the mines and this I did under the emergency regulations. I gave the mine owners 28 days' written notice to move their equipment and workers out of the area; anyone seen in the area after that date would be shot on sight.

During this period curfews were in operation throughout the district from 6.30 p.m. to 6.30 a.m. – the hours of darkness. From 5 a.m. to 6.25 a.m. on the 24th April 1951 Police Lieutenant Evans and I, backed up by a section of constables, had a curfew check on the Mawai and Johore Bahru roads. We arrested 22 people for breaking the curfew. All were in possession of identity cards and were summarily dealt with.

On 5th May 1951 Sisek Tin Mines reported that the wooden palongs at the mine, about a mile from the police post, had been set on fire by terrorists. From 5.05 p.m. to 5.55 p.m. I flew over the area in an Auster aircraft again piloted by an army sergeant. After flying around the mine and seeing the damaged palong and satisfying myself that the police were alright – they were out, waving – I took it that we would be returning to Kota Tinggi, but this army sergeant had other ideas. After making another circle of the mine, he dived on to the police station and I saw policemen scattering in all directions. I was not feeling too well when he pulled out of the dive; I thought that that would be the end of it, but no, he made another dive on the station and then set off for Kota Tinggi.

When we got down to the river he was flying the aircraft between the trees on both sides of the river and when we were passing the Kota Tinggi police station on the river bank he had to rise to get over the bridge outside the station. When he dropped me off on the football field he looked at me and said, 'You don't look too bad.' Others he had had up must have looked worse. The interesting thing about flying with these sergeants was that you had to read the map and point out the way to go. The following day, 6th May 1951, police from Sisek Tin Mines called at Kota Tinggi police station; when I asked them how far the aircraft was from the roof of their station, they replied 'Duo kaki' (two feet).

At 7.45 a.m. on Thursday 17th May 1951 I left Kota Tinggi police station on a visit to Mawai, Kuala Sedili and Kambau police stations. I had three constables as an escort and was travelling in a police Chevrolet truck. The Mawai police station was only 10 miles from Kota Tinggi and situated on the Sedili River. It was not uncommon for vehicles travelling this short distance to come under fire from terrorists at the 5th milestone which was a jungle-covered hill on the right of the road. On rounding a bend 8 miles from Kota Tinggi and 2 miles from Mawai police station there was a wire across the road. As there were no red flags and no warning of any description we assumed an ambush, stopped and dived into the ditches on either side of the road. It was then we heard an engine running, similar to that of a tractor; moving along the ditches we found that the wire was being used by loggers to pull logs out of the jungle. Five Chinese males were present. They were all arrested, taken to the Mawai police station and charged with obstructing the highway.

At 9.30 a.m. the four of us embarked on a hired launch at Mawai and proceeded down the river to Kuala Sedili, arriving at the Kuala Sedili police station at 11.30 a.m. The Malay sergeant in charge of the Kuala Sedili police station had a problem on his hands. Wild dogs had chased a deer into the sea and it had swum out so far that it became absolutely exhausted. A Malay fisherman came on the deer and as it was almost gone he cut its throat and pulled the deer aboard his sampan (Malay boat). He came ashore and reported the matter to the police because the deer in Johore State are royal deer, the property of the Sultan of Johore, and no one dare interfere with them. Their status is similar to that of swans in this country. I got on the radio to Haji Abdul Kadir bin Haji Hassan, head of the CID in Kota Tinggi, and related the facts to him. He radioed back later stating that the Sultan had given his blessing to the people of Kuala Sedili and ordered that the meat be shared amongst the villagers. The station sergeant said that he would have his share and that I would have a meal with him on my return from Kambau. In the meantime he boiled up two turtle eggs for me which were very good.

A grim episode

At 2 p.m. the three constables and I left Kuala Sedili for Kambau, again travelling by launch. At 3 p.m., when about halfway up the Kambau river, we were ambushed. The Kambau river is very narrow in certain stretches and at such places it is necessary to slow down to allow the boatman in the bow of the launch to pole the launch around some of the bends. There were hills on both sides of us where the ambush was set and because the river was narrow here it was difficult to make out if you were being fired on from one side or both sides of the river. I returned fire to the right-hand side of the river, which turned out to be correct on later investigation. We were almost out of the ambush, rounding a bend, when a burst of bren gun fire struck the engine and knocked it out of commission. As the river was fast flowing the launch was drifting back into the centre of the ambush area. I told my men to get out and make for the river bank. As I was jumping off the gunwale of the boat I was hit in the back, my hands opened up automatically and I lost my American .300 carbine in the river.

I got to the bank with another constable who had lost his .303 rifle in the river. The bank of the river turned out to be a mangrove swamp with mangled almost impenetrable roots. After getting into the swamp I discovered that I had also been hit in the knee, left side and right arm as well as in the back. With the constable, I struggled through the tangled mangrove trees and roots away from the ambush position. While doing so, I felt something tugging at my right shoulder. This was my lanyard which was attached to my 9 mm Browning automatic pistol. I always carried this pistol attached to my belt on the left side of my body with the butt facing my right hand as it was easier to draw quickly from that position. A terrorist bullet had struck the top of the magazine inserted in the butt of the pistol; two rounds had exploded in the magazine and severed my Sam Browne belt. The thing tugging behind was my pistol, still attached to the lanyard on my shoulder. I picked up the pistol but found that it would not operate. After struggling through the swamp for about 100 yards I saw that I was losing a lot of blood, so I decided not to go any further.

I told the constable, who was with me and unharmed, to follow the river for about 3 miles and that he would reach Kambau police station by doing so. There was no point in him staying with me. After he left, the terrorists came down from the hill and searched the area for about 45 minutes. I could hear them clearly speaking in Chinese; they were only a matter of 20 yards away at times. I was almost submerged in 2 feet of water with dense undergrowth all around me. I then heard explosions and these turned out to be the terrorists sinking the launch with grenades. The other two constables and two boatmen went to the other side of the river. One constable had a finger shot off and the head boatman was wounded in the side. After the explosion everything went quiet. I was never unconscious and must have fitfully dozed off now and again.

Occasionally small fish would nibble away at the raw flesh on my knee but otherwise I spent a long but uneventful night.

At 9 a.m. on the morning of 18th May 1951 a bugle sounded and I took it that the terrorists would be moving off as the security forces were bound to follow up the ambush. The two constables and the two boatmen who went to the other side of the river made their way down the river bank and eventually came upon a Malay village. They borrowed a sampan from the village and made their way to Kuala Sedili where they arrived just before 10 p.m. They reported to the station sergeant that I and one constable were missing. The station sergeant reported the incident by radio to Kota Tinggi police station. It was decided to wait until daylight before investigating the incident. A combined military (Malay regiment) and police party under the command of Fred Lewis, superintendent of police and officer in charge of a police jungle company, along with the two constables who they picked up on the way, headed for the ambush area in an armoured launch which belonged to the Kambau rubber estate. I was pleased to hear the steady throb of the motorboat engine as it drew nearer.

Suddenly machine guns opened up and bullets were flying over the area where I was lying. The two constables had accurately pointed out the ambush position and, fearing that terrorists may still be in position, had opened up to see if there was any reaction. As the motor boat was passing my position I gave a loud blast on my police whistle. The boat eased off and I was delighted to hear the voice of Fred Lewis. He shouted 'Is that you Jock?'

I replied 'Yes.'

'Keep blowing your whistle and we will soon have you out of there.'

Fred was dressed in jungle-green trousers, jungle boots and police beret. He was bare from the waist upwards.

I was soon on board the launch and had first aid administered to my wounds. The time was 12.30 p.m. I was taken to

94

Mawai by launch where a military jeep-type ambulance was waiting and I was taken to the general hospital, Johore Bahru, arriving there at 6 p.m. On arrival at the hospital I was put into a single officers' ward and immediately my jungle-green uniform was cut off with scissors. I was given two small brown tablets and then had my wounds dressed. My wounds consisted of two bullet wounds across the back, one wound left side which had also gone through the magazine of my pistol, wound on knee cap of right knee and flesh wound of right arm.

For the next 10 days my wounds were dressed morning and night. About half an hour before a start was made on the wounds I was given two small brown tablets by a nurse. The flesh around the wounds was septic and almost gangrenous because of the humidity and the fact that the wounds had not been treated for 27 hours. To clean them up the nurse put crystals into the wounds, similar to salt, which apparently burnt out the rotten flesh. This was fairly painful and I found out later that the small brown tablets I was being given were morphine tablets. After 10 days had elapsed the surgeon, Mr Yeoh Bock Choon, stopped the issue of morphine tablets. What a state I was in that night. My temperature shot up to over 104 degrees. The nurses had to change my pyjamas twice and I had ice packs on my head. The following morning when the surgeon was doing his rounds I pleaded with him to give me some more morphine tablets. He said that he could not and the reason that I had had such a bad night was that I had almost become addicted to the drug. He added, however, that I would get sleeping tablets at night. Before the day sister went off duty at 9 p.m. she came in with two sleeping tablets which I took right away. At about 9.15 p.m. the night sister came in with another two sleeping tablets which I also had. Apparently the day sister omitted to enter the issue of sleeping tablets on my chart for which I was most grateful. The sleeping tablets took me over the addiction and I had no further craving for the morphine.

A few days after being admitted to hospital I was visited by my brother David, a police lieutenant stationed at Kuala Lipis in Pahang State. He volunteered a blood transfusion but the surgeon said that he would pick me up much faster on iron, a thick syrupy medicine which I received twice a day. My blood count on entering hospital was only 30, but after a month it had risen to 95. After being in hospital for about 4 weeks the surgeon decided that the 10-inch wound below my shoulder blades should be stitched and that this would be done under anaesthetic. I was told during his morning visit that I would not get dinner that night (usually at 6.30 p.m.) and that I could not eat anything until after the operation the following day. At 6.30 p.m., the night before the operation, a nurse came in pushing a trolley with a lovely evening meal. I took it for granted that the surgeon had put off the operation. I enjoyed the meal and the trolley was taken away. About 7.30 p.m. a young Malay nurse came into my room pushing a trolley on which was situated a large basin, an enamelled ewer, a length of rubber hose and a jug. She then told me that I should not have had the meal and the equipment she had with her was to make sure that I did not keep it for too long. Needless to say the soapy water worked like a miracle.

About a week after this during the regular morning visit from the surgeon, he told me that he was going to try to skin graft my right knee. Standing at the bottom of the bed with the surgeon was the day sister and a nurse. His instructions to his staff were to shave my right thigh, wash it thoroughly with ether and bandage the area with a wide sterile bandage for 3 days. About an hour later the nurse came in, shaved my *left* thigh, washed it thoroughly with ether and bandaged it with a wide sterile bandage. Three days had elapsed when, during the surgeon's morning visit, he said, 'I'll have a look at your knee.' When taking the bandage off my knee he said, 'Didn't the nurse shave your right thigh?'

'No,' I said, 'but my left thigh has been shaved, washed and bandaged.'

He passed some derogatory remark and said that he did not want to cripple me entirely. Following this my right thigh was shaved, sterilised and bandaged and I had to wait a further 3 days for the skin graft operation. I could see clearly how the mistake had been made. Standing at the bottom of the bed my left leg would be on their right. The service, attention and the food in the hospital were all excellent. Every evening during my 7 weeks and 3 days' stay in hospital I had alternate visits from Chief Police Officer, P. H. D. Jackson, and Deputy Chief Police Officer, Jack Masefield; and every morning I had alternate visits from their wives. Jack Masefield was a close relative of the poet laureate, John Masefield, and supplied me with all my reading material – books such as Viscount Cunningham's autobiography, *A Sailor's Odyssey*, Popski's *Private Army*, etc. I was amazed to find that all the books supplied to me had been read by my Chinese surgeon, Mr Yeoh Bock Choon.

After I'd been in hospital for 2 days I was allowed visitors; the first group numbered over thirty, the majority being traders and government officers from Kota Tinggi. On 21st May 1951 I had a visit from George Patterson, the administrative officer from Kota Tinggi who was also the senior magistrate. He had been to Singapore and, when passing a newspaper shop, had seen a large notice from the *Straits Times* on a billboard which stated: 'K. TINGGI OCPD SHOT'. He removed it from the billboard and presented it to me in hospital.

I had another visit from George Patterson in early June 1951 when he handed me a cutting from the *Daily Telegraph* dated 31st May 1951. This was an article to the editor of the newspaper by T. W. Lilley from Welling in Kent. Tom Lilley was the officer from whom I took over the Kota Tinggi district in October 1950. The final paragraph of the article reads as follows:

There is still another urgent necessity; it is that the British Government should make available the equipment for

97

ensuring a reasonable measure of protection for the fighting personnel in Malaya. In the same issue as that in which General Martin's article appeared you recorded an ambush and consequent wounding of my successor as officer in charge of the police district of Kota Tinggi in Johore. I assert that had he been in a boat more suitable for the task, instead of a partially armoured boat, he would probably not have been ambushed at all.

The true facts were that I and my party of policemen were not even in a partially armoured launch. The only partially armoured launch in the area belonged to the Kambau rubber estate and the only time I travelled in this launch was when being transported to hospital after being ambushed and wounded. The only launches at our disposal were 15 to 20 feet long, and all belonged to local people, mainly Chinese; these vessels were hired by the police whenever required. They were open launches with seats across, and were crewed by two people, the coxswain and bowman. The owners of these launches never refused a hire although their lives were at risk all the time. They were the unsung heroes.

The vehicles we had at the time were again almost all soft-skin vehicles, the majority being American Chevrolet troop carriers. When stationed at Kota Tinggi I had only two armoured personnel carriers at my disposal. They were protected with sheet steel all around but were open on the top. When travelling through hilly country they were not the best type of transport to use. Terrorists shooting down from high vantage points could create havoc with bullets ricocheting around inside the steel box.

I had regular visitors every Thursday evening in the form of Mr and Mrs Chow Eng Kwai. Mr Chow Eng Kwai, a tin miner from Singapore, was the owner of one of the mines at Susor Rotan which I closed down a month or so before I was ambushed. He obviously did not hold this against me and always brought a massive bag of fruit which was shared throughout the hospital. They were all very kind and genuine people. I was discharged from hospital on 9th July 1951 and was granted 2 weeks' sick leave. This I spent with Mr and Mrs Peter Law; Peter was then working at police headquarters, Johore Bahru, having previously been the officer in charge of the Mersing police district.

From paperwork to film-work

On 23rd July 1951 I took up the post of personnel officer at police headquarters, Johore, working directly under the deputy chief police officer, Jack Masefield. As far as the English language was concerned Jack was a perfectionist, as I soon learnt. All outgoing letters of any consequence had to be passed to Jack for approval and seldom if ever did one get through without red alterations. From 23rd July until 6th August I had to attend hospital for $1\frac{1}{2}$ hours' physiotherapy treatment each day and thereafter every second day until 25th August.

On 10th September 1951 I was given an additional job in connection with the direction of manpower. Apart from officers in the special branch and criminal investigation department, members of the Chinese community were loath to join the regular police. As a result of this the government introduced the Direction of Manpower Act which meant that young Chinese males could be called up to serve for 2 years in the police force. My job was to travel throughout the state of Johore with four constables to document and measure all those called up, after which they were medically examined. Fifty conscripts were ordered to appear at each call-up centre but I never found 50 conscripts awaiting my arrival – more frequently only half of that number. There were a number of reasons for this:

(1) Young Chinese males did not fancy a police career and preferred to work as rubber tappers, tin miners,

loggers, etc., where they could make much more money and have fewer restrictions.

(2)   Their parents were subject to intimidation by the Min Yuen (masses movement) which supported the communist insurrection, in which case the son was advised by his parents to move from the area.

(3)   Some were supporters of the terrorist campaign and these, when conscripted to fight on the side of the government, joined the terrorists in the jungle instead.

Between the 10th September and the 16th October 1951 I visited the following centres on a number of occasions to document and measure up the conscripts who attended each centre: Johore Bahru, Segamat, Pontian, Batu Pahat, Kota Tinggi and Muar. When the terrorists heard about the Direction of Manpower Act they were furious and did their utmost with propaganda to destroy the government's initiative by ambushing and murdering government personnel involved in the work. To this end at 2.30 p.m. on the afternoon of the 16th September 1951 at the 14th milestone on the Johore Bahru to Pontian road my party came under fire from terrorists from the left hand side of the road when we were returning to Johore Bahru by Land-Rover. Fortunately the fire was inaccurate and no one was injured. Only 6 days had elapsed since I had started the job. After that we travelled to as many centres as possible by rail although there was no guarantee that the train would not be attacked and derailed – a fairly frequent occurrence in the Malaya of 1950 and 1951.

On 17th October 1951 I was given another job – that of technical adviser to the American film company Metro Goldwyn Meyer, who were making a film in Malay on the emergency. The film was mainly shot in an area of jungle on the north side of Singapore island. My job was to advise on police dress in jungle warfare, construction of a terrorist camp and supply suitable personnel to fire live ammunition from bren guns, etc; this I did until my departure on leave to the United Kingdom on 28th November 1951.

Prior to going on leave I was informed by contingent special branch headquarters, Johore, that terrorist documents recovered from a terrorist camp in the Kota Tinggi district revealed that the terrorists who ambushed my party on the 17th May 1951 had camped on the jungle-covered river bank for 15 days, knowing that I would come that way sometime. The documents also revealed that, as officer in charge of the Kota Tinggi police district, I was held responsible for the deaths of four of their number who had been killed at Kampong Lukut on the 6th March 1951.

Happier Times

At 11 a.m. on 28th November 1951 I boarded SS *Carthage*, a P & O liner, at Singapore docks. At 12.15 p.m. SS *Carthage* pulled out from the docks en route to the United Kingdom, calling at Penang, Colombo, Bombay, Aden, Port Suez, Port Said, Algiers and Tilbury, London, arriving there on 19th December 1951. All officers going on leave to the United Kingdom were given first class passages by the Malayan government. After getting settled in I went to the dining room to find that I was sharing a table for six. I was delighted to find that two of my table companions were well known to me, namely: Haji Abdul Kadir bin Haji Hassan, head of the CID when I was stationed at Kota Tinggi, and James McNab, the officer in charge of the Kulai police district. The others were two British rubber planters and a Malay assistant superintendent of police. Haji Abdul Kadir and the Malay ASP were on their way to a police college in the United Kingdom on a six months' course.

When travelling through the Mediterranean in December we encountered very stormy weather, as evidenced by the lack of passengers turning up for meals. On one particular day

101

there were only 50 passengers in the first class dining room instead of 250. All six were present at our table. The ship was pitching continually and everyone was looking very green. The table steward asked what I wanted for lunch and I ordered a cold salad. It was soon apparent that my table companions were also feeling very sick; all ordered the cold salad. One concentrated on holding on to the plate of food and picking off bits of salad here and there; there was little or no conversation. Occasionally the odd individual would be seen peeling away from tables and heading up to the open deck.

At this point I thought we would have to have a make-or-break situation. I asked my table companions if they had heard the story about the two tinkers in the north of Scotland who were caught up in a blizzard. All said that they hadn't heard this one. I then went on to say that the two tinkers, complete with packs, had been making their way from one village to another when they were caught in the blizzard. 'They were cold and hungry', I continued, 'and took shelter behind a clump of trees. One of the tinkers was foraging around and came upon the carcase of a dead cat. He picked it up and started eating into it . . .'

At this point two of my table companions shot away from the table and up the stairs.

'The tinker eating into the carcase then asked his mate if he would like some, which he declined . . .'

One more away.

'After the one tinker had satiated himself they set off again along the road. They had not travelled very far when the tinker who had eaten a part of the cat stopped and was violently sick and vomited on the road . . .'

Another table companion vanished, leaving Haji Abdul Kadir as sole survivor of the story. Continuing, I said, 'The tinker who declined to eat a piece of the cat earlier got down on his hands and knees and licked up the vomit off the road. His friend then asked him why he had declined to accept a piece of the cat when he offered it earlier. His reply was that he preferred a warm meal . . .'

At this point poor Haji Abdul Kadir had to give in; he pushed his chair back and in his rush to get up the stairs knocked over the chief steward, who was standing at the door behind our table, supervising the other stewards.

After all that commotion I felt fine – but didn't I get a hard time when I ventured on deck?

After docking at Tilbury and clearing customs I made my way to the Orkney Islands, arriving on Friday 21st December 1951. The following letter from Breezy Eason, Director of the Metro Goldwyn Meyer film company, was awaiting my arrival.

Sea View Hotel,
Singapore
8th December 1951

Dear Bill,

I received a little note from Syed Alwi Alhady explaining that he had had the pleasure of your company on his trip to Penang; he expressed great pleasure in having you with him during the short run. We were all very much disappointed in missing a little get together with you before you left. Mike explained that you were in the Chicken Inn with the Hennessy's while we were at the bar. I was sorry that you didn't make your presence known to us. I cannot tell you how much you were liked by all the members of the company; it would be good for your ears to hear their high and sincere praises of you.

I do hope that your long journey home will be a pleasant one, and trust that you will enjoy an association with your old acquaintances and relatives and have a good well-earned leave. I cannot thank you too much for the technical help you gave our production. We consider ourselves very fortunate in having a man of your background and real experience in action with the banditry in Malaya. Your experiences in bandit combat were an inspiration to all those who knew of them; how you ever came through alive will always remain a mystery but let us just say that God must have had a hand in it. The good fact remains that you are alive and apparently none the worse for wear – and that, my boy, is something we are all very happy about.

So please, let us hear from you, Bill old boy, and if you ever hit the good old United States I would like to have you visit me at my home in the San Fernando Valley. The address is:

12709 Kling Street,
North Hollywood,
California.

With best wishes and kindest regards from Bert, Mike, Lou, Tom, Jim, Glenn and Mary and all the gang.
I beg to remain
Yours very respectfully,

Breezy Eason

An engaging homecoming

On Saturday evening, 22nd December, I called at the Bellevue Hotel, St Margarets Hope, to meet friends and acquaintances. Saturday evening in those days was the night when all farmers came to the village to shop and do other business and finally ended up in the pub to discuss general farm matters. I was welcomed like a long-lost friend, having been away for 3 years and 4 months, and was plied with drink before I could get a chance to go to the bar. When I eventually got to the bar, the barman, John Omand, said, 'This is yours.' He pointed to 13 nips of whisky and 13 bottles of McEwans export. I gave him a fiver and told him to give everyone a drink in the bar.

A strange but pleasant custom used to exist in those days. It was fairly common practice for a farmer to go up to the bar, order a round of drinks for his drinking companions and then add: 'And one for the constable.' This was in no way a form of bribery and in fact showed appreciation for the work being done by the constable. In the Bellevue Hotel there was a small secluded shelf where the constables' nips were placed and it was not uncommon on a Saturday evening to see four or five nips on the shelf.

Having been away for so long I was granted 6 months' leave on full pay and had to report to the colonial office medical specialist in Leith to get an assessment of my fitness to return to full duty in Malaya. After being home for 2 months I got to know my future wife, Lena Norquay, who was working with my sister Lily and her husband, Willie Smith, in the St Margarets Hope cafe. After I had been on leave for 5 months the Leith medical specialist sent me to specialists in Harley Street, London. Their main concern was the state of my knee. I was granted 2 months' extension of leave on full pay and had to report back after that time to Leith. This I did on a further two occasions and was granted a further 2 months' extension after the second visit and a further 1 months' leave after the third visit. Following the third visit the specialist passed me fit for sedentary duties.

In August 1952 I got engaged to my fiancée, Lena, and on 2nd November I left Orkney by air for Malaya. I was told to report for duty at police headquarters, Bluff Road, Kuala Lumpur.

I arrived in Kuala Lumpur on 7th November and was posted as the police representative on the director of operations' staff at police headquarters. I was accommodated in the police headquarters mess at Venning Road, Kuala Lumpur. This was a large, rambling wooden building on stilts with verandahs all around – a pleasant and airy place.

My work was in the research section of the director of

operations and my immediate boss was Colonel Cruikshanks. This work turned out to be fascinating. All units operating throughout Malaya had to submit returns on all terrorist incidents and details of all terrorist camps which they had come across during their operations. Details submitted included type of terrain, e.g., primary jungle, secondary jungle, swamp, lallang; position of camp above sea level; distance from nearest river/stream; distance of sentry posts from the camp, and how many; and condition of food, particularly tinned food, e.g., milk, meat and fish. In addition if contact was made with the terrorists at or near the camp we needed to know how many were killed and wounded, what type of weapons were used and how many rounds fired. All this information was researched and the details punched on cards. By putting all the cards into the machine and punching in the relevant information it was possible, on a country-wide basis, to establish the average positioning of camps above sea level, the distance of sentry posts from the camp (this depended on the type of terrain where the camp was located), distance of rivers or streams from camp, etc. The two most effective weapons in the jungle proved to be the Greenyer automatic shotgun and the .300 American carbine. The life of tinned food cached in the jungle was 6 months.

During May and June 1953 30 police constables and I acted as escort to a loudspeaker company from England carrying out field tests with equipment blasting messages into the jungle. Apart from protecting the technicians and their equipment we were also required to go into the jungle on a compass bearing with one of the technicians to test the effect of the loudspeakers with a decibel measuring machine. In dense jungle it was found that messages were unreadable at 1000 yards and therefore useless in the propaganda war to effect the surrender of terrorists. At the same time tests were being carried out with loudspeakers from the air; by contrast this proved very effective and was used to great effect by surrendered or captured terrorists to call on their comrades in the jungle to surrender.

The ground-based equipment was put to good use by resettlement officers when moving squatters from crown land on the fringes of the jungle and resettling them in new villages. The equipment was also used to disseminate government policy and the fight against terrorism to the isolated villages throughout Malaya.

As the work on the director of operations' staff was coming to an end I was asked if I was interested in joining the special branch. I said I was, and in July 1953 attended a month's special branch course at special branch headquarters, Kuala Lumpur. The course was designed to find out if people were suitable material for the special branch. On completing the course I was accepted. I was then attached to a research unit at police headquarters, putting together dossiers on all top brass in the Malayan Communist Party: its secretary general, all members of the central executive committee and all state committee members.

In the meantime, I had been writing to Lena and she had agreed that we would get married in Kuala Lumpur on 10th October 1953. When passing on the news to her parents she was told by her father: 'No one but a damn fool would go so far, and if you get there send a telegram!'

The farthest Lena had travelled before taking on this mammoth safari was a visit to Aberdeen for a yellow fever injection. I met her at Kallang Airport, Singapore, on 2nd October 1953. We stayed overnight at the Railway Hotel, Singapore and the next day took the train to Kuala Lumpur. Waiting to meet us at the Kuala Lumpur railway station were Colonel and Mrs Lakin who very kindly offered to put Lena up until the wedding. Colonel Lakin was in charge of the psychological warfare section on the director of operations' staff; among other things he was responsible for broadcasting to terrorists from the air.

Special memories of Penang Island

The wedding was held at St Andrew's Church, Kuala Lumpur, and the reception in the police mess; everything went off without a hitch. Mrs Lakin was matron of honour and Bill Cound, assistant superintendent of police (a brother officer), was the best man. Lena was given away by Colonel Lakin. Present at the wedding were two Orcadians. The first was Alex Sutherland, with whom I had tied for the book describing the island of Penang all those years ago in 1939. Alex was married to the manager of a rubber estate in the district of Klang, Selangor state. The other was Bill Omand, a lance corporal in the military police then stationed in Kuala Lumpur. After the reception we left on honeymoon to the Lone Pine Hotel, Penang, 250 miles from Kuala Lumpur. We spent a very pleasant 2 weeks in Penang, travelling all over the island with its beautiful beaches for swimming or sunbathing. There were also a large number of crystal clear pools in the hills of Penang where one could get a very cool dip.

A trip on the Penang hill railway is a must when in Penang. The hill railway is worked on a cable system in two stages. When the carriages leave the bottom of the hill to a point halfway up the hill carriages from the halfway point descend on the same cable. This is an endless cable. At the halfway point passengers disembark and join the second stage which works in an identical system and on the upward section this takes you to the top of the hill over 2723 feet above sea level. From the top of the hill one has an excellent view of Georgetown, the capital, and all of the island lying below. This is particularly beautiful at night when all the lights are on.

After the honeymoon we returned to Kuala Lumpur, where I was notified that I was being transferred to the special branch at police headquarters, Johore state. We stayed overnight at a Chinese hotel in Kuala Lumpur and the following morning left by road for Johore Bahru. On arriving at police headquarters, I was notified that there was no government accommodation available and that we had in the meantime been booked into the Gleneagles Hotel, Singapore. This was a pleasant hotel situated in a quiet area of Singapore near the botanical gardens. The Malayan government paid the accommodation charges. On reporting for work the following day I was notified that I had been appointed case officer in the special branch and that I had a staff of three Chinese inspectors, two male and one female.

The case officer's job was to build up projects mainly concerned with penetrating the Malayan Communist Party in the jungle. One of the priorities was to identify couriers who operated between district and state committees in the jungle. Some of these couriers lived in the open as rubber tappers, tin miners, etc. It was extremely difficult to identify couriers but we occasionally got a break through the interrogation of important surrendered terrorists or through documents found on killed or captured terrorists. One such identified courier lived in a village in North Johore. It was a small village and any strangers in the village would have been spotted immediately. We had to use some pretext to get the courier away from the village. This entailed gathering details of his family and close associates. During research into his family it was discovered that his wife had gone back to China and at that time if the wife of a Chinese male did not return within a 6-month period the immigration authorities had the power to refuse entry.

A check with the immigration authorities revealed that the courier's wife had in fact been out of the country for over 6 months; with the approval of the head of special branch the immigration authorities therefore agreed to write to the courier about his wife's immigration status and invite him to Johore Bahru for an interview. By this time, apart from the three Chinese inspectors on my staff I also had a clandestine force of surrendered terrorists – male and female – who lived in safe houses in the town of Johore Bahru. It was arranged that on the arrival of the courier at the immigration office I would visit another immigration officer in the same large office. When the courier had completed his interview, the courier would be identified to me and I would follow him out of the building. Outside the building I had a surveillance squad of three surrendered terrorists together with one Chinese inspector. When I emerged from the building I gave a pre-arranged sign that the Chinese male I was following was the courier. I then dropped out of the scene.

The three members of the surveillance team followed the courier from the immigration offices on a hill and headed for the town of Johore Bahru. One of the team, a surrendered MCP branch committee member, got chatting to the courier on the way down the road. His approach was that they had met somewhere before in north Johore, and when nearing a coffee shop he invited the courier to join him in a cup of coffee and a chat. The courier said that he did not want coffee and appeared to be suspicious, on which the ex-MCP man grabbed hold of him while the other two surveillance team members moved in. During the struggle the courier's watch fell to the ground.

By this time two of the Sultan of Johore's bodyguards had appeared on the scene, as had the Chinese Inspector Feng Yeh Kim, a brilliant officer. He told the bodyguards that the man being held had attempted to snatch a watch and that they should help put the man in his (the inspector's) car. This they did before retiring from the scene. The three others left for a safe house so that the courier could be interrogated by the inspector and myself. After 4 hours the courier was won over and he agreed to carry on with his job as courier for the terrorists; after special arrangements had been made regarding the leaving of messages and contact points, he was released and got the night train back to north Johore so as not to arouse suspicions about his absence. The courier turned out to be a very useful agent and supplied valuable information to the special branch.

After being in Singapore for 6 months, travelling to and

from work daily – a distance of 52 miles return, for which I was paid a mileage allowance – I was beginning to get tired of travelling through the heavy traffic and asked the housing authorities in Johore Bahru to rent a house in Johore Bahru for myself and my wife. This they refused to do although I pointed out to them that I could rent a house for a lot less than they were paying for my accommodation in the Gleneagles Hotel together with the mileage allowance. Getting nowhere with them, I took the matter into my own hands and moved into a new bungalow which I rented from a well-to-do Chinese for 400 Malayan dollars a month (about £53.00 at that time). When I got my first bill from the bungalow's owner I sent it to federal headquarters in Kuala Lumpur with a covering letter explaining that the housing department in Johore Bahru would not allow me to rent a house in Johore although by doing so I was saving the treasury over 100 dollars a month in accommodation and mileage charges. Although I was rebuked for going against regulations the treasury agreed that I was right and it did make sense.

By this time (mid–1954) the security forces were getting the upper hand in their struggles against the terrorists and a gradual rundown of the police force commenced. Every British officer under 30 years of age – I was in that category – was given options to transfer to other overseas territories. When I received the offer I could not opt for any of the territories as I was still officially graded down for office work and one had to be fit to get a transfer to another territory. I replied accordingly. A few weeks later I was offered a transfer to Tanganyika subject to my being passed fit. I arranged for a medical board with my surgeon, Mr Yeoh, and he passed me as fit but said that he would not guarantee my knee for ever. It was my intention to go direct to Tanganyika from Malaya to complete the last 6 months of my tour and as a result my wife left for the United Kingdom on the P & O liner *Chusan* on the 10th August 1954.

I moved out of the rented accommodation and moved

111

into the police mess. When talking to brother officers in the mess they asked why I had not gone to the United Kingdom on leave first before transferring to Tanganyika. I said that I thought it better to have a brief stay myself first to find out conditions, particularly the availability of housing. It was then pointed out to me that if I went direct to Tanganyika the 2 years' leave earned in Malaya would be paid at Tanganyika rates of pay which were considerably lower than those of Malaya. This I did not believe and was told to write to the personnel department, police headquarters, Kuala Lumpur. I did this, and the personnel department confirmed that if I went direct to Tanganyika when I eventually went on leave my leave earned in Malaya would definitely be paid at the Tanganyika rates of pay. I wrote back immediately and told the personnel department that I now wanted to take my leave prior to going to Tanganyika. This was in order and without much warning I was booked to the United Kingdom by air on 15th September 1954. So I arrived in the UK 2 weeks after my wife's arrival.

VI

Tanganyika Police

Dar es Salaam

Our leave came to an end on 13th January 1955 and we left London for Dar es Salaam, Tanganyika (now Tanzania) on *MV Warwick Castle* of the Union Castle Line. On the way out we called at Gibraltar, Marseilles, Genoa, Port Said, Port Suez, Aden, Mombasa, Tanga and Dar es Salaam. We arrived in Dar es Salaam on the morning of 13th February 1955 and were met on board and welcomed to Tanganyika by a police officer from the personnel department. Accommodation was arranged for us in the Maison Blanche Hotel, about 3 miles from the city centre. The room allocated to us was on the ground floor adjacent to the bar. Apart from the noise, the room was airless and hot, there was no air conditioning, and, what with our having to use mosquito nets at night, the conditions were anything but tolerable.

On reporting to police headquarters I was informed that I was to take over the European and Asian desk at special branch headquarters. These headquarters were situated on their own in an old German fort near the Avalon cinema in the centre of town. This was a very dark and dingy building; all the windows were barred and the concrete floor of my ground-level office had no carpets or other fineries. The post involved a lot of information gathering and writing on the political aspirations of leaders in the Asian community and, to a lesser degree, Europeans. Applications for naturalisation were also processed through the office; such applications were building up at that time because the Asians and non-British Europeans were unsure of their future under a forthcoming African government. So there was much interviewing of referees and checking of assets, bank accounts, houses, property, etc. Another part of the job was to vet (for suitability) films which the cinemas intended to screen. I was one of a panel on the official censor board. Asian films were screened by a similar board but in my place my Asian inspector, Raza Qureshi, attended. Protection of visiting Asian and European VIPs also came under our umbrella.

For the first time in my police career I was faced with having to dictate letters, reports, etc. I did not have a personal secretary and was told that either Mrs Barton or Mrs R. O. Wemban-Smith would do my work. The one available on my trial run was Mrs Wemban-Smith and she turned out to be the wife of the director of establishments, a very senior civil servant. I explained to Mrs Wemban-Smith that I had never dictated before and that she would have to bear with me. On the third day she said, 'You are doing fine,' and added as a bit of encouragement that my predecessor used to drive her up the wall.

'Why?' I said.

'Because when he was ready to dictate letters or reports he got up from his desk and, with his hands clasped behind his back, paced back and forth across the floor, dictating sentences now and again. After every two sentences he asked me to read it back. The pacing back and forth really got on my nerves.'

This boosted my ego and I never looked back from there on. After spending 3 weeks at the Maison Blanche Hotel we moved out on our own to a second-floor room of the Metropole Hotel in town, and then notified the treasury. Financially it did not affect the treasury because no matter what hotel

114

accommodation you stayed in the government only paid 20 shillings a day towards accommodation costs. We moved into the Metropole on 4th March and on the 18th March were allocated a government quarter in Kinondoni Village, about 3 miles from the city centre.

My wife, Lena, got a post in the treasury keeping the accounts of the provident fund schemes for the local African and Asian government servants. Later, on behalf of the Tanganyika Society for the Prevention of Cruelty to Animals, she took over the Kinondoni Kennels from Mrs Thain, who had gone on 2 months' leave to South Africa. Lena cycled the mile from our government quarter to the kennels every day. One morning on her way to work she heard a strange sound coming from the side of the path. On checking she came across a tiny bush baby whose mother had been killed. She took the bush baby home and nursed it, feeding it initially with milk using the inside of a fountain pen. The bush baby, which was kept in the spare bedroom, slept all day but became very active at night. Between the bedrooms about a foot from the ceiling there was fine wire mosquito netting and at night the bush baby made quite a noise running along this netting.

After we had had the bush baby for 3 or 4 weeks I had a visit from Mr and Mrs John Golding. John was the provincial special branch officer for Tanga Province. Lena was at the kennels when they called. They were fascinated with the bush baby and as they had a large secluded garden in Tanga and were prepared to build a house for the bush baby I handed the animal over to them. When Lena returned from work I told her what I had done. She was to say the least not at all pleased but I felt that it was better for the bush baby.

During weekends my wife and I strolled along the lovely beaches at Oyster Bay and Bagamoyo on the coast of the Indian Ocean. The temperature averaged 80°F but it was very pleasant with the ocean breezes. When beach combing we picked up lovely shells which we still have. Most of these were cowrie shells which have beautiful coloured patterns and are glazed like porcelain. Being a newcomer to a new country, one had to study and pass the law and language examinations of that country.

Arusha, Northern Province

After spending just over a year in Dar es Salaam I was posted to Arusha, capital of the Northern Province of Tanganyika, as provincial special branch officer. We left Dar es Salaam by train at 12.30 p.m. on 7th April 1956 and arrived at Dodoma, the capital of the Central Province, at 6.25 a.m. on the following day. My vehicle, which was following by goods train, had not arrived so we had to spend the night of 8th April in the Dodoma Railway Hotel. At 7.45 a.m. next morning we left by road for Arusha. At 11 a.m. we stopped off at Kondoa to visit Mr Tulloch, the Kondoa district officer. We resumed our journey to Arusha at 12.45 p.m. and arrived at Arusha at 6.50 p.m. At that time (1956) there were only a few hundred miles of tarmac throughout Tanganyika. All other roads were made up of a red laterite material and in the dry weather the dust clouds raised by the vehicles went everywhere. At the end of a long journey one was very grimy.

On arriving in Arusha we were accommodated in the New Arusha Hotel. At that time the population of the town which covered an area of $2^1/_2$ square miles was in the region of 10 000 people. The town was situated 4500 feet above sea level on the lower slopes of Mount Meru, an impressive mountain whose stark peak reaches 14 979 feet, making it one of the highest in Africa. The average temperatures made the place very pleasant. In the cool season the temperatures during the day hover between 55° and 70°F while in the hot season they are from 60° to 80°F. The moderate temperatures made it a healthy and invigorating place in which to live. After getting settled in the hotel we were visited by Mr and Mrs Charles Sutcliffe. I had arrived to take over the province from Charles who was due to take vacation leave.

The northern province of Tanganyika, roughly the size of Scotland, comprised six districts: Arusha, Moshi, Monduli, Mbulu, Singida and Kondoa. The governor's representative in the province was the provincial commissioner while each district came under the jurisdiction of a district commissioner assisted by one or more district officers, depending on the size and population of the district. The district commissioners were responsible to the provincial commissioner. The police organisation was set up on similar lines, the provincial police commander being stationed at the provincial capital with the provincial commissioner and officers in charge of the police who were stationed at every district headquarters. The provincial special branch officer was stationed at the provincial headquarters; he was responsible for informing the provincial commissioner, provincial police commander, district commissioners, district officers and officers in charge of police about what was going on in their respective areas in the fields of political and trade union activity and anything else which could create problems for them in the future. In this connection, intelligence reports were distributed at the end of every month, one copy going to the director of special branch.

From 9th to 18th April 1956 I was fully involved in taking over from Charles Sutcliffe; this included meeting all his intelligence sources and all government officials in the area. (At the end of this period I was admitted to the Arusha hospital with an ingrowing toenail; Dr McGill operated on this and cut a section away. I was discharged from hospital on 25th April.)

On 30th April we took over No. 76 Lodge Road, Arusha, the government quarter vacated by the Sutcliffes. After getting organised in the house I set off on a tour of part of the province from 5th to 15th May. Miss Pat Quinlan, my secretary, was left to look after the office until I returned. I was accompanied by a detective corporal as well as my cook, who rustled up meals when I stayed in government rest houses. During this 1000-mile safari we visited Singida, Ndugutu, Mkalama, Kisiriri, Kiomboi, Iranodol, Kinampanda, Shelui, Ilongero, Kyoja, Kondoa and Hambi before returning to Arusha. To keep in touch with the various district officials one had to spend at least ten days in every month on safari.

The elderly cook I had at this time enjoyed coming on safari with me. He also liked a drop of whisky and used to help himself to an odd drink when we were not around. To put a stop to this I put a definite mark on a bottle of whisky which was about half empty. I turned the half empty bottle upside down and put a clear mark showing the level of whisky in the bottle. When the bottle was then placed the correct way up the mark was about an inch below the level of whisky in the bottle. The cook apparently noted the mark on the bottle and drank the quantity of whisky to bring it down to the mark. When I called him in and explained and demonstrated that I had put the mark on the bottle when the bottle was upside down, his face fell and he admitted that he had had an odd drink. On 2nd June 1956 I went to Monduli, about 50 miles from Arusha, to see the district commissioner of Masailand, Mr Francis Townsend. Masailand district covered by far the largest area of the northern province, from Ibibo in the south to the Kenya border in the north.

On 14th June 1956 I left Arusha for Loliondo near the Tanganyika/Kenya border. This was a journey of 200 miles. On the way one passed through the town of Mto Wa Mbu (mosquito creek) which nestles at the foot of the escarpment near the Ngoro Ngoro crater. The high water tables at Mto Wa Mbu created flourishing market gardens around the town. After Mto Wa Mbu one started climbing to the top of the Ngoro Ngoro crater, 5000 feet above sea level. The crater has been described as the eighth wonder of the world. It covers an area of 100 square miles with walls 2000 feet high. It is the largest intact crater on earth. One then descends to the Serengeti plain and climbs again to Loliondo. The area from Ngoro Ngoro to Loliondo was teeming with wildlife. We arrived at Loliondo at 5 p.m. to find that the district officer was away on safari. On 15th June I conferred with Mike Leaf, the stock prevention officer. Mike's job was to prevent the rustling of cattle by the Masai tribesmen – a way of life to them. At the time, he and the district officer were concerned with Mau Mau activity on the border; he produced Mau Mau documents found in the border area. At 8 a.m. on the 17th June I left Loliondo for Arusha, arriving at 7 p.m. On 2nd July, after the Mau Mau documents had been delivered to special branch headquarters, Nairobi, Kenya, I attended a conference with special branch officers at Ngong in Kenya to discuss Mau Mau problems in the border area. Mr Diges La Touche, the provincial police commander, Northern Province, also attended the meeting.

On 8th August 1956 I received a signal from the police at Loliondo stating that an armed Mau Mau terrorist had been captured in the border area. I left Arusha for Loliondo at 12.30 p.m. My African driver had just returned from a 3-month mechanics' course and we were in possession of a brand-new long-wheelbase Land-Rover. To get to Loliondo without refuelling – there was no guarantee that you would get petrol on the way – one had to leave with a full tank of 14 gallons of petrol plus a further 10 gallons in two army-type jerry cans. On setting off from Arusha I noted that the choke light kept coming on, illuminated green. I drew the driver's attention to this; he gave the knob a bang and the light would go off for a few miles and then come on again. I also mentioned to the driver that the vehicle appeared to be sluggish. He assured me that everything was alright, and who was I to argue with a trained mechanic?

On entering the Serengeti plains the petrol tank ran dry. I pointed out to the driver that we should have travelled much further than this on the tank of petrol and that something must be wrong. He assured me that there was nothing wrong. We emptied the two jerry cans in the tank and set off again. After crossing the Serengeti plain one begins to climb and eventually reach a height of 8000 feet above sea level at Loliondo. At 9.30 p.m. we ran out of petrol with 25 miles still

119

to go; we were then over 6000 feet above sea level. I said to the driver we would have to walk into Loliondo and leave my elderly African cook to look after the vehicle. As there were all types of game in the area – elephants, lions, buffalo, wildebeest, etc. – the driver was absolutely petrified and refused to accompany me. My cook volunteered to come along. I was armed with a .38 snub-nose Smith & Wesson pistol. We plodded on and encountered plenty of game on the way but they fortunately ignored us, as we did them.

At 4.40 a.m. on 9th August we entered Loliondo where I knocked up Mike Leaf, who produced a very welcome cup of coffee. After having a rest and arranging accommodation for my cook, Mike Leaf and I went to the local Loliondo petrol station, filled up two jerry cans and, in Mike's Land-Rover, set off to recover my Land-Rover. After putting the petrol in the tank, Mike checked the engine and found that the choke mechanism had jammed and that we had in fact driven all the way from Arusha with the choke fully open. The type of choke on the Land-Rover at that time was inclined to lock fully open if you pulled the choke out hard, and it would not unlock by pushing the choke in, as my driver had been doing all day. I dealt with him later.

We got back to Loliondo at 7 a.m., and from 8 a.m. to 10 a.m. I had discussions with the special branch officer from Ngong, Kenya and with Andrew Clarke, assistant superintendent of police, also from the Kenya Police. From 10 a.m. to 11.30 a.m. and from 2 p.m. to 4 p.m. we interrogated the captured Mau Mau terrorist, Kimani s/o Karanja. On the following day interrogation continued from 10 a.m. until midday and from 2 p.m. to 3 p.m. At 7.30 a.m. on the 11th August (my wife's birthday) I left Loliondo for Arusha with the prisoner. At 4.05 p.m. I arrived at Arusha and handed over the prisoner's possessions to Colin Brown, assistant superintendent of police at the Arusha police station; the prisoner I handed over to the Arusha prison authorities.

The terrorist had been armed with a very dilapidated Lee

Enfield rifle with a homemade bolt and firing pin. It seemed a very unsafe weapon to fire but to prove in court that it was a lethal weapon and capable of firing bullets we had to try it out on the range. To do this we fixed the rifle in a clamp, attached a string to the trigger and from a safe distance pulled the string. It did work and that was all that was required for the court. On the 12th August 1956, the day after returning from Loliondo, I gave my driver a one-way bus and rail warrant transferring him from Arusha to Dar es Salaam and told him to report to special branch headquarters on arrival. When the bus had departed I telephoned my boss and told him about my highly trained mechanic and what I had done about him. My boss was absolutely furious but took no further action.

On 17th August 1956 Lena gave birth to a baby girl whom we named Heather. I went to visit Lena during the evening of the first day and on entering the ward was met by Dr McGill who stopped me and would not let me go any further. He said, 'Before you see your wife go down to the duka (shop) and buy 12 bottles of stout to build up her strength and then you can go in and see your wife.' I dutifully complied.

When Lena was first seen by Dr McGill in the maternity ward he asked her where she came from. Lena replied that she came from a place that he, the doctor, had probably never heard of. To her surprise, he mentioned that he had been stationed at the Lyness naval base on the island of Hoy in the Orkney Islands for 5 years during the war. He was then a medical officer in the Royal Navy. After the visit to the hospital I went home, but I was not alone for very long. The first to call was Mr Digges La Touche, carrying a bottle of whisky. He was followed by Miss Pat Quinlan and Colin Brown; a few others dropped in to join in the celebrations.

Because of the forthcoming visit of Her Royal Highness Princess Margaret to Arusha on 15th October 1956, I was involved (during the latter part of September and up to 14th October) in screening personnel working in premises to be visited by HRH. The princess and her party flew into Arusha from Dar es Salaam at 3.50 p.m. on the afternoon of 15th October and moved directly to the governor's lodge, just outside the town where she and her entourage stayed during their visit to the northern province. I was introduced to Superintendent Crocker from the Metropolitan police, HRH's personal bodyguard, who advised me that once in the lodge he was no longer responsible for HRH's security and that it was over to me. Regular police were posted on all roads and tracks leading to the governor's lodge and special branch detectives were discreetly placed around the grounds of the lodge.

Anyone living in the area of the lodge who had to use the roads to get to and from their houses were supposed to be issued with passes. Our house, No. 76 Lodge Road, was a few hundred yards behind the governor's lodge. On the morning of 16th October my wife put Heather, our daughter, in her pram and went through the police checkpoint on her way to the shops. On the way back she was stopped by the police on duty and told that she couldn't go past that point. As the police on duty could not speak English and as Lena's standard of Kiswahili was not yet very good, a stalemate occurred. She finally got through to the police that her home was up the road and that her husband was the special branch bwana (master). The police on the checkpoint still would not let them through and with the field telephone called up the police station and asked me to come and vouch for her. This I did and there was no further trouble.

Superintendent Crocker was a regular visitor to our house, dropping in for coffee in the morning or dropping in to bath Heather while my wife made the coffee. When Superintendent Crocker found out that we came from Orkney he said, 'I had a choice of going on the trip to Tanganyika with HRH Princess Margaret or going to Orkney with the Queen Mother. I elected to go to Tanganyika and here in Tanganyika I meet Orcadians!'

On 16th October HRH attended a 3-hour-long baraza (large tribal gathering) held on the Arusha golf course, and on the following evening she attended a reception and dinner at the Arusha school from 5.30 p.m. to 10 p.m.

At 8.30 a.m. on 18th October I was on duty at Moshi where HRH and her party attended the Moshi show before visiting the Kilimanjaro Cooperative Union premises. The Princess left Moshi for Nairobi en route to the United Kingdom at midday. After she had departed all police officers on duty had drinks and lunch in the police mess at the Moshi police training school. At 6 p.m. I drove Superintendent Geoffrey Popple, deputy head of the special branch, to the airport; he was returning to Dar es Salaam. Geoff and his wife, Vera, had stayed with us in Arusha during Princess Margaret's visit. I then returned to the police mess and had further drinks, and a number of us went to Moshi town for a meal.

Coming in from Arusha to the outskirts of Moshi I had to negotiate a roundabout and when going from the police training school to the town centre I had to negotiate another roundabout. When leaving the hotel in Moshi at around 1 a.m. I was slightly under the weather but negotiated the roundabout with no trouble. I was heading for Arusha, over 50 miles away, and was travelling at around 50 m.p.h. in a Morris Minor. I had forgotten all about the second roundabout which suddenly loomed up in front of me. I had no time to stop and mounted the 6-inch kerb around the roundabout, stopping about 12 feet from a lamp standard at its centre. There were no street lights in the area, just the one light in the centre of the roundabout. In the distance I saw a vehicle following so I backed off the roundabout and headed in the direction of Arusha. The vehicle which I had seen in my mirror went around the roundabout and headed off in a different direction.

I then decided that I had better stop and check my vehicle. I found that both the stabilisers on the steering mechanism had snapped and there was a deep cut in the offside front tyre. I drove home at around 40 m.p.h. Apart from the possibility of getting a puncture one had to be on the lookout all the time for game crossing the road. I eventually got home at 3 a.m. and found myself locked out. I called my wife but got no response. My wife was quite naturally furious because I should have been home at around 8 p.m. and I hadn't called her to let her know what was going on. At that time we were looking after a dog for one of our neighbours. I made my way around the house checking windows and found the top section of the bathroom window on the latch. The area I had to get in through measured 30 inches by 12 inches and this I accomplished with very little trouble – must have been sober. In the bathroom, wagging his tail, was the dog; he hadn't barked once.

On 22nd October 1956 my wife and I visited Mr and Mrs Jim Cameron, who had a farm at Ol Joro about 20 miles outside Arusha. They were a delightful couple. They grew maize and sunflowers. From the latter they obtained pyrethrum. Jean Cameron baked all her own bread and made her own soap. When on tour on 10th November 1956 – a Saturday night – I stayed in the Singida Hotel. Here I met two Irishmen who were Brothers at the Chem Chem Catholic Mission about 60 miles from Singida. They enjoyed their beer and we spent a pleasant evening chatting. As I was going to Ndugutu the following day and as they were waiting for a lift to Chem Chem, which was on the way, I offered to take them back to the mission. We left at 8.45 a.m. and arrived at the mission at 1 p.m. (poor roads). There I met Father Ryan and was welcomed like a long lost friend. He asked, 'How long are you going to stay with us? A week? Two weeks?'

I said, 'No, I am going on to Ndugutu and will be staying in a rest house there.'

Father Ryan insisted that I had lunch with them, which I did, and which I thoroughly enjoyed. They were wonderful characters. Their mission, their accommodation, school, outhouses, etc., had all been built from scratch, including the making of all the bricks used in the buildings. I left the mission at 2 p.m. and spent the night at Ndugutu.

On 19th March 1957 I had to appear in the magistrates' court, Arusha with Kimani s/o Karanja the captured Mau Mau terrorist. He was remanded to the high court. During the trial of Kimani in the Arusha high court on the 27th March Kimani kept interrupting the proceedings of the court and at the end of the trial Judge Abernethy said to Kimani, 'If you had been a reasonable man and had not kept interrupting the proceedings I would have given you 5 years' imprisonment, instead of which I sentence you to 10 years' imprisonment, the maximum.'

On the morning of 31st May 1957 I helped my wife to pack and then drove her to the Arusha airport en route to Nairobi and the United Kingdom. As my end-of-tour leave was not due to come up until late October Lena and I thought it better that she go home with Heather in the summer to get acclimatised before winter set in.

On the Move Again

On 3rd June 1957 I was notified that as I had only 4 months to go before going to the United Kingdom on leave I was being transferred to Moshi, 50 miles away, to relieve Arthur Croneen, the special branch officer there who was about to take home leave. After handing over the Arusha office to Norman Brend on 20th June 1957 I went on transfer to Moshi. I spent a pleasant 4 months in the Moshi area and was again blessed with a very able and efficient secretary, Mrs C. J. Strong. Her husband was an official with the Tanganyika Electric Supply Company (TANESCO).

On 17th October 1957 I left Moshi by air for Nairobi and London after handing over the Moshi office to Graham Sharp, assistant superintendent of police. I was on leave from 18th October 1957 until 5th March 1958. The first 2 months we spent with Lena's parents at the farm of Barebreck, South Ronaldsay. We then moved into the cafe in St Margarets Hope which belonged to my sister and brother-in-law, Lily and Willie

Smith, and which was closed at the time. As our leave took in Christmas and New Year I had occasion to visit my father at 6 p.m. on New Year's Eve. My mother was away at the time looking after my sister's children, she being in hospital having another child. This particular New Year's Eve was a beautiful evening; there was a slight covering of snow on the roads with a hard sparkling frost and a full moon. When entering the kitchen of my father's house I was surprised to see him working on a shoe on a last. I passed the remark, 'You are surely not mending shoes on New Year's Eve?'

He replied, 'Hell, no, I am hammering in frosts in the shoes.'

The reason became clear then. He was preparing for a night out in the pub; the frosts in the shoes would prevent him from slipping. I left him at his important work and invited him to dinner and drinks with us around midday the following day. He arrived at the cafe at midday and stayed with us until 9 p.m. I was walking him home and when about to pass the Murray Arms Hotel, he said, 'I'll branch off here,' and went straight across the street into the pub, leaving me standing in the street. I went home.

At about 2.30 a.m. on the morning of 2nd January, neighbours of my father called to let us know that they had picked up my father at 2 a.m. about a mile from the village going 'first footing'. They took him home but he couldn't find the key to get into the house, which was normally hidden in an outhouse; so they called on us to get help. I went with my father and neighbours to the house and failed to find the key. Knowing that one of the front windows was not latched and that there was a settee directly below the window I opened the window and we got my father in that way; but we pulled down all the curtains as well. After seeing that my father got to bed and after re-erecting the curtains I went home. When my mother returned a few days later she spotted that something had happened to the curtains but mum was the word.

On 5th March 1958 we left London for Dar es Salaam on

MV Dunnotter Castle of the Union Castle Line. We followed the same route and called at the same ports as had the *Warwick Castle* in 1955. Heather, our daughter, contracted measles half-way through the voyage and was put into isolation in the ship's hospital. When we arrived in Dar es Salaam on 3rd April 1958 a police launch came alongside the liner and took us ashore so that Heather would not come into contact with the other passengers. We were taken straight to No. 40 Ada Estate, Oyster Bay, Dar es Salaam – a house just vacated by Mr Edwards, an assistant superintendent of police. As was normal when moving into houses in Tanganyika, the neighbour called with an ice cold bottle of water. Water in Dar es Salaam had to be boiled and filtered before drinking. The neighbour who called turned out to be an Orcadian, a Mrs Jean Thomson. Her husband, Jim, worked for the government printers, Dar es Salaam – a small world. After getting settled in I was notified that I was to join P. L. Connolly DFC, assistant superintendent of police, who was in charge of the Dar es Salaam special branch unit.

On 2nd May 1958 commissioner of police Mr R. E. Foulgar retired and was replaced by Mr Geoffrey S. Wilson.

On 13th August 1958 I was called to the office of Ian Paton, assistant commissioner of police, director of special branch, who told me that I was being sent to Mwanza in the Lake Province to find out what was going on there. He said that reports from the special branch officer there were unclear, but it was apparent that the populace were being encouraged by politicians to refuse to comply with such government regulations as those requiring them to have their cotton crops treated against pests and their cattle inoculated against the deadly disease of rinderpest. Reports were also being received that the police motorised company (riot police) were having to contain hundreds of rioters.

Early on the morning of the 15th August I left by air for Mwanza on the direction of the commissioner of police. I was met at Mwanza airport by the special branch officer for the

127

Lake Province who took me to the Mwanza Hotel. After booking in and putting my effects in my room I went down to the bar, as requested by my host. As my host was the same rank as myself, a senior assistant superintendent of police, I had to tread warily. We talked and drank beer until 12.30 p.m. then had lunch. After lunch my host invited me back to the bar.

I said, 'Hadn't we better go to the office to see what is going on?'

He reluctantly agreed. The special branch office was only a 5-minute walk from the hotel.

'What is happening in the province?' I asked.

'Certain politicians are encouraging people to refuse to comply with government regulations and are agitating the population to oppose everything the government stands for. In this connection large crowds suddenly appear in areas like the football ground. Sometimes there are a few hundred, sometimes two thousand. Up to date the motorised company (riot police) have contained all the trouble without a serious incident.'

'How and when did this all start,' I asked, 'there must have been a starting point?'

He pointed to his in tray which was stacked high with reports from his special branch detectives.

'I'll have a look at these,' I said.

My host's reply was, 'OK, I'll see you later,' and he walked out of the office.

I went through the pile, the majority of the reports being in Kiswahili, and when I got to the bottom of the tray, the oldest report was dated April 1958. The trouble had started in Geita district in April 1958 when a local Tanganyika African National Union official, contrary to the union's territorial policy, started agitating the people against government regulations with a view to speeding up self-government.

I stayed in the Mwanza area for 2 weeks, translating all the reports. In this I was helped by a very able African detective, sub-inspector Anicett, who spoke reasonably good English. I spent 3 days of the 2 weeks in Geita district and spoke at length with the district officer stationed there. Finally I produced a 28-page report covering the period April to 3rd September 1958. I returned to Dar es Salaam on 5th September and handed the report over to Ian Paton, director of special branch. Immediately after this I went down with malaria, having contracted it in Geita district; I was off work for a week.

Lake Province

While at home in bed I had a visit from Ian Paton who told me that the provincial commissioner and the provincial police commander were demanding the removal of the special branch officer from Mwanza, Lake Province, and that he wanted me to go and take over the province. As I was getting over the bout of malaria I agreed to do it and told my wife Lena. At the time she was almost 8 months' pregnant with our second child. We vacated our house, No. 40 Ada Estate, on 15th September and stayed that night in the New Africa Hotel, Dar Es Salaam. We left the city by rail at midday on 16th September and arrived at the Mwanza railway station at 10.30 a.m. on the 17th. We were met at the station by the Lake Province special branch officer and were taken to the Mwanza Hotel where we were accommodated until 27th September – the day on which the Lake Province special branch officer was transferred to Dar es Salaam. We took over his quarter, 15 Capri Point, Mwanza, on the following day.

The Lake Province was similar to the Northern Province in that it was made up of six districts: Mwanza, Geita, Shinyanga, Maswa, Musoma and Tarime, the headquarters being at Mwanza, the third largest town in Tanganyika. Mwanza lies on a narrow peninsula jutting out into Lake Victoria, the second largest freshwater lake in the world. Lake Victoria is 3717 feet above sea level and is comparable in size to Scotland. Ships from Mwanza carry goods and passengers to Bukoba and

Musoma, the two main towns on the Tanganyika shores of Lake Victoria. The tribe who lived around Mwanza, the Sukuma, were the largest tribe in Tanganyika, about 2 000 000 strong in the 1960s. The majority of the Sukuma tribe were farmers growing maize and cassava and rearing cattle. Cotton was widely grown as a cash crop.

After getting settled in I found that although I had a detective staff of 16 constables and other ranks, not one of them could speak Sukuma. At the same time information was received that illegal meetings were being held throughout the province, an area the size of Scotland, and that at these illegal meetings farmers who were complying with government regulations were being arraigned before illegal courts (set up during these meetings) and were being fined a bullock, or the equivalent price of such; they were also ostracised by the rest of the community by being denied the right to draw water from the communal well or purchase anything from the local shops.

I went to see the senior assistant commissioner of police, Lake Province, Mr H. E. Moore, and put my problem to him, i.e., that I had no Sukuma-speaking detectives and could he provide help temporarily.

'How many men do you need?' he asked.

'Four constables.'

'Right, you shall have them today.'

After a week's basic special branch training I sent these four constables out with one or two trained special branch detectives to try and find out where and when illegal meetings were being held. After 2 weeks they came across an illegal meeting being held under a number of baobab trees about a mile from a local village. The constables and detectives were all dressed like locals and squatted down to listen. Their task was to obtain the name of the headman of the area and the name or names of the people who convened the illegal meeting, the illegal magistrates who were officiating and those fined for complying with government regulations.

After the meeting they had to make their way back to Mwanza with all speed. To assist them they were given sufficient funds to travel by bus and if convenient and unobtrusive were dropped off and picked up later by special branch Land-Rovers.

After attending the first meeting our people had no further problems in attending future meetings because the conveners of the illegal meeting always announced where and when the next meeting was to be held. When my men returned during the evening – any time between 7 p.m. and midnight – I had to debrief them, and obtain all the relevant names. I then called on Basil Elkington, the Mwanza district superintendent of police, and Andy Barclay, superintendent of police and officer in charge of the motorised company (riot police), and passed on the information to them. They organised a police party, went to the area of the illegal meeting, and found out where the headman lived. Getting him out of bed, they obtained knowledge of the whereabouts of the people who convened the illegal meeting and those who acted as illegal magistrates; they called at their houses and arrested them. Also obtained were statements from the people who had been fined by the illegal court. Those arrested were taken back to Mwanza and locked up in the police station for the remainder of the night/morning; they appeared in the magistrates' court at 8 a.m. charged with holding illegal meetings and usurping government power by acting as illegal magistrates.

This attempt to intimidate the local population and usurp government power went on for a year and out of a total of 105 arrests, not one pleaded not guilty. The accused could not fathom out how they had been found out and talked about witchcraft. Sentences over the period varied from a £5.00 fine to 5 years' imprisonment. Every morning at 9 a.m. during this difficult period I had to attend a meeting in the provincial commissioner's office and report on the previous day's happenings. Present on these occasions were the senior assistant commissioner of police; staff officer, police; district commissioners from the Mwanza urban and rural districts; and the superintendent of police, Mwanza district. After 3 months of long days and nights – 7 a.m. to midnight or later – the provincial commissioner remarked one morning, 'Mathieson – you are not looking well.'

'It is little wonder,' I said. 'I am getting very little rest as I have to translate all the reports I get and then write them out in longhand for my two copy typists, all of which takes time.

'You should have a stenographer on your staff,' he said.

I replied, 'That is correct.'

'Why haven't you got one?'

I replied that my predecessor would not dictate reports so headquarters took the stenographer away.

'What have you done about it?' asked the provincial commissioner.

'I have been on to my boss, Ian Paton, ever since I was posted to Mwanza – I have had promises but nothing has transpired.'

The provincial commissioner, Mr S. A. Walden, the most senior provincial commissioner in Tanganyika at the time, picked up the phone and rang the Chief Secretary to the Governor, Mr Grattan-Bellew and said, 'My special branch officer in the Lake Province hasn't got a stenographer – do something about it.' Mr Grattan-Bellew rang up my boss and asked him why I hadn't got a stenographer.

When I got back to my office the phone rang. It was Ian Paton. 'Why have you gone behind my back?' he asked.

I said I had not; pressure of work was making me ill, a fact which the provincial commissioner had noted, and anyway I had on a number of occasions asked for a stenographer but had had to live on promises. The next day I went to Mwanza airport to pick up Miss Maureen Kelly, stenographer.

During this hectic time our son Peter was born on 30th October 1958. On Monday 7th November 1958 I had to attend

132

the magistrates' court, Mwanza, with our houseboy, John s/o Patrick. He had a drink problem, and when it came to drinking my whisky and then watering it down this was too much for me. On the Saturday afternoon (5th November) he had come back to the house around teatime, having been to the pombe market (local beer market), and had a fairly good dram in. I was not in the house when he returned but he asked my wife for a sub. As he had already had a sub that week my wife refused to give him another advance. I returned at that moment and agreed with my wife. The houseboy went away and a short time later we heard the tinkle of bottles from the dining room area. I went through and caught the houseboy with the bottle of whisky in his mouth. I took him and the bottle to the police station where he was locked up for the weekend.

When analysed, the whisky was found to have been watered down, obviously at an earlier date.

After I had given evidence the magistrate asked the accused if he had anything to say. He called me a liar. The magistrate then sentenced him to one year's imprisonment. I thought this very harsh. Later the same day the probation officer called at my office to get the balance of his wages and when I said I thought the sentence very severe for drinking and watering down whisky, the probation officer informed me that this was the sixth time the accused had been charged with 'stealing by servant'.

At the end of January 1959 my stenographer Miss Maureen Kelly returned to Dar es Salaam and her place was taken by Miss Jean Foggo.

Promotion
During a meeting with the provincial commissioner in early 1959 he said that the provincial special branch officer, Lake Province, was down on the establishment list as a superintendent of police and asked why I didn't have this rank. I said

that I was too junior an officer (in age and service) to be a superintendent.

He said, 'If you are doing the job well, as you are, then you should have the rank.'

I am positive that Mr S. A. Walden did something about this because on 1st July 1959 I was promoted to superintendent of police.

At this time, owing to overwork, I became run down to such an extent that my legs broke out in sores – the doctor called it septicaemia.

On 16th May 1959 Mr H. E. Moore, senior assistant commissioner of police, retired and was replaced by Len Harvey, assistant commissioner of police, as the provincial police commander. I cannot speak too highly of the unstinting support which I received from Mr Moore.

On 9th July 1959 I had a visit from the director of special branch, Mr Ian Paton. On Ian's return to Dar es Salaam he sent the following note:

Dear Jock,
I write to thank you for your kindness and attention both to Mr Watson and myself during our recent visit. I know it must have been quite a strain for you as you were obviously not feeling very well at the time. My regards to your wife and, again, thank you very much.
Yours sincerely,
Ian Paton

At the time of Ian's visit my promotion had not yet been promulgated. I was notified of this promotion on 6th August by the deputy commissioner of police.

Dear Mathieson,
I send my warmest congratulations to you on your promotion to superintendent and I am delighted that your good work in the past has been recognised. I know that

you will continue to give of your best in the increased responsibilities which this rank demands.
With best wishes to you for your future happiness.
Kind Regards.
D. W. Humphrey.

On 18th October 1959 we moved house from 15 Capri Point, Mwanza, to 75 Myakabungo, Mwanza.

On 3rd November 1959 I had a visit from the commissioner of police, Mr Geoffrey Wilson. He was taken to the special branch office by Mr Len Harvey, assistant commissioner of police, the provincial police commander.

The first thing Mr Wilson asked was, 'How are your Malayan wounds doing?' Like all good senior officers, he had obviously had my personal file out before he went on tour. A sundowner (cocktail party) was held that evening in the special constables' club to welcome the commissioner, to which all police officers, special police officers and their wives were invited. During the sundowner the commissioner of police sought out my wife and when talking to her asked if she would like a transfer out of the area. My wife's reply was that she was quite happy where she was but if there was a transfer in the offing then it would be better to ask her husband. The commissioner of police did not ask me if I wanted a transfer; this was his way of finding out whether my wife was agitating for a move and whether this might be getting me down. There was nothing further from the truth. My wife supported me wholeheartedly through that hectic year in Mwanza and it was sheer overload of work and long hours that was wearing me down.

On his return to headquarters in Dar es Salaam, the commissioner must have come to the conclusion that the work in the Lake Province was too much for one special branch officer because in January 1960 I had an African assistant superintendent of police posted to me to look after the districts of Musoma and Tarime in the north of the province. He was Amri Kweyamba, a very able officer who took a load off my shoulders. On 6th February I was given another officer to assist me with the work in the province. He was Eric Gray, assistant superintendent of police, a very welcome addition to the Mwanza special branch office. About the same time Petro (Peter) Bwimbo, an African chief inspector, was added to the Mwanza office. He was an intelligent and delightful personality.

On 8th February 1960 a new secretary arrived in the person of Miss Barbara Ross. Miss Jean Foggo proceeded on leave on the 13th February 1960. By this time we had taken care of all the anti-government problems in the province and work had become routine. On 10th August our third child, Lorna, was born in Mwanza hospital.

On 26th August 1960 I had a visit from the new director of special branch, Mike Hannington. Mike had taken over the hot seat from Ian Paton who went on transfer to Uganda as head of the special branch there.

From 22nd September until 10th October 1960 I was on casual leave, the provincial special branch problems being left in the capable hands of Eric Gray.

Vivid memories of Serengeti National Park

While we were stationed in Mwanza, the Holdsworth family were great friends of ours. Bill Holdsworth, assistant superintendent of police, was the deputy boss of the motorised company (which dealt with disturbances such as demonstrations, strikes and riots) and had formerly served in the Palestine police force. His wife Rosetta came from Israel. At the time of my casual leave their daughter Mary arrived on a visit from Malaya, her four-year-old son having been killed when he ran across a road in Malacca. Mary's husband was a captain in the army. As Mary was quite naturally very depressed we arranged to go on a week's visit to the Serengeti National Park. Mr Len Harvey, the provincial police commander, very kindly gave us his long-wheelbase station wagon Land-Rover. We were accommodated in rest houses adjacent to the game warden's house in the north of the Serengeti plain, situated about 40 miles east of the Musoma road. We saw lots of game but during our short visit our son, Peter, contracted scarlet fever; this kept my wife and I in or near the rest camp.

On returning to Mwanza we decided to return by what was called the corridor, a rough track through the middle of the plain; we travelled in a southerly direction for 60 miles and then west to the Musoma/Mwanza road. At about midday we were travelling at about 15 m.p.h. through tall grass (3–4 ft high) when suddenly we ended up at a 45 degree angle, the track having been washed away overnight by a flash flood. The sudden impact without any warning resulted in a number of injuries. My wife's leg was badly gashed and I received a beautiful black eye. Lorna, our daughter, who was sleeping in a suitcase at the rear of the Land-Rover was catapulted out of the suitcase but Bill Holdsworth grabbed one of her legs before she could hit the windscreen; this fortunately saved her from any injuries. The remainder of the party escaped injury. The nose of the Land-Rover was 6 feet below the level of the track. As there was no hope of getting the vehicle out that day, and no hope of anyone coming by, Bill Holdsworth and I started the mammoth task of trying to recover the Land-Rover. To do so we hunted around for dead trees and branches which we placed under the chassis of the Land-Rover; we then jacked up the Land-Rover a few inches before inserting another tree or branch, and so on. When we were working at this the women got a wood fire going and brewed up tea.

The water after the flash flood was very brown and muddy and to overcome this problem my wife produced a muslin nappy and strained the muddy water through the muslin. In the meantime Bill Holdsworth and I struggled away, jacking up the vehicle. The problem we had initially was that the ground under the Land-Rover was soft and when pressure was put on the jack it pushed the tree/branch into the soft ground. We laboured away until darkness settled around us at 7 p.m. and then all moved into the vehicle to get away from swarms

137

of mosquitos. We spent a very uncomfortable night with the Land-Rover still embedded in the bank at a steep angle. As soon as daylight broke, Bill and I got back to work and at around 1 p.m. we succeeded in jacking up the Land-Rover to a stage where it was level with the ground around us. Our hands were raw and bleeding with the effort. We set off again and found that the track through the corridor was flooded to a depth of 12 inches. As we did not know what further hazards were ahead of us we took it in turns at running in front of the Land-Rover for about 2 miles until we reached higher ground. At the time a small spotter plane flew over looking for us as we should have returned the previous evening. At around 3 p.m. we came out on to the main Mwanza/Musoma road and headed back to Mwanza, where we arrived at dusk.

I returned to work from local leave on the 11th October 1960 and from then up to the end of March 1961, when we left on vacation leave for the United Kingdom, nothing of any particular significance occurred. Work became routine and there were no further anti-government troubles. Prior to departing on leave I received the following letter from Mr Len Harvey, assistant commissioner of police, the provincial police commander for the Lake Province:

Dear Jock,
May I take the opportunity of thanking you for all you have done to help me here during the last 2 years, particularly during the 'troubles'. It has been of great assistance to know that one could always rely implicitly on the information provided by the provincial special branch and I know very well just how much this happy state of affairs is due to your own personal efforts. I hope you will both have a very pleasant leave and that we shall see more of each other when you return.
Yours Aye
Len Harvey

On 30th March 1961 we vacated our quarters and stayed that night in the Mwanza Hotel. Next day we left Mwanza by air for Entebbe in Uganda and then went on to the United Kingdom on flight BA 162Y on end-of-tour leave. In June 1961, while on leave, we purchased a small cottage and 3 acres of land known as Daisybank on the island of Burray. At one auction sale in Stromness we fully furnished the cottage for the sum of £25.00 and a short time later we moved in.

A New Challenge Coincides with Tanganyikan Independence

On 23rd September we returned to Dar es Salaam by air. This time we were accompanied by my 17-year-old daughter Shirley, from a previous marriage. We were allocated government quarter No. 14, Bongoyo Road, Oyster Bay, Dar es Salaam. I was posted to special branch headquarters and appointed head of the operational section. Shirley, in the meantime, got a post with Stewarts Stores, Acacia Avenue, Dar es Salaam – a high class general store catering for almost everything. On 1st December 1961 I was promoted senior superintendent of police and appointed deputy director of special branch.

Tanganyika was granted independence on 9th December 1961. From 26th February 1962 to 3rd March 1962 I carried out inspections of the special branch stations at Iringa, Mbeya, Mtwara and Lindi. As some of the leading politicians in the Tanganyika African National Union, including some government ministers, were disgruntled at the slow pace of Africanisation of the police, prisons and immigration services, government changed overnight, with the loss of our very moderate minister for home affairs, George Kahama, and the prime minister Julius Nyerere. Nyerere was replaced by a 'yes' man called Rashidi Kawawa and we got as our minister for home affairs Oscar Kambona, who had spent 4 years in Czechoslovakia and was naturally quite leftish.

After the change in Government, Africanisation was speeded up. Mr. M. M. E. Shaidi, the only African superintendent in the force, was appointed commissioner of police. Amelia Mzena, the only assistant superintendent of police stationed at special branch headquarters, Dar es Salaam, was appointed director of special branch. One senior assistant commissioner of police was kept to advise M. M. E. Shaidi but all other top ranks of the police from commissioner down to senior superintendents were Africanised. All the superintendents – the backbone of the force – were kept on. This was a clever move. The superintendents could go if they wanted to do so but would forfeit their pension rights.

At the end of May 1962 I was notified that my post was being Africanised on 14th June. As it was impossible to get accommodation on any of the Union Castle liners going out of Dar es Salaam and as it was forbidden to sell our vehicle in Tanganyika or anywhere else in southern Africa, we decided to drive to Cape Town and get a passage back to the UK from there. To ensure that we did not sell our car en route a deposit of £75.00 had to be left with the Standard Bank of South Africa, Dar es Salaam, which was returned on proof that the vehicle had been exported to the United Kingdom.

VII

Home

Cape Town via Victoria Falls

On 17th June 1962 we left Dar es Salaam on our way to Cape Town, covering 5500 miles en route. Our first stop was Mbeya, the capital of the southern highlands province of Tanganyika. We travelled via Morogoro, Kilosa and Iringa to Mbeya – a distance of 500 miles from Dar es Salaam. Mbeya is situated 5300 feet above sea level. We stayed overnight in a thatched roof rest house in Mbeya. On the morning of 18th June we left Mbeya and crossed the border into Northern Rhodesia (now Zambia) at Tunduma, 73 miles from Mbeya. After travelling 305 miles on laterite roads we stopped at Mpika and spent the night there. We left Mpika on the morning of 19th June and travelled on to Kapiri Mposhi – a distance of 259 miles – staying overnight in a motel. On 20th June we left Kapiri Mposhi on the 422 mile journey to Livingstone. We had to have two tyres replaced in Lusaka on the way. We stayed in Livingstone on 20th and 21st June where we visited the Victoria Falls, Livingstone Memorial and the Victoria Falls bridge.

The falls are very impressive. They are at their most spectacular during the months of April and May when the Zambezi river is at its height, but the great clouds of spray often obscure the giant falls of water. When we visited the falls in June it appeared to be the perfect time for viewing. The Victoria Falls are situated 750 miles from the source of the 1725-mile

Zambezi river. The river rises in Zambia, passes through a part of Angola, and, after forming the boundary between Zambia and Zimbabwe (at that time Northern and Southern Rhodesia) flows through Mozambique into the Indian Ocean at Chinde, 975 miles from the falls. The maximum width of the falls is 1860 yards, over a mile, and their mean height is 304 feet. They are twice as high and one and a half times as wide as Niagara. The maximum flow over the falls, reached in April and May, is estimated at 75 000 000 gallons per minute. The minimum flow, in November and December, is about 3 250 000 gallons per minute. The Victoria Falls are 2900 feet above sea level.

The Victoria Falls Railway Bridge was first built in 1905 by the Cleveland Bridge and Engineering Company, Darlington, England. A road was added and the bridge converted to single track railway by the same company in 1930. The length of the bridge is 219 yards, its weight being 1868 tons. The height of the railway and road bridge above high water is 355 feet (411 feet at low water).

On 22nd June we left Livingstone and moved on to the Wankie National Park, just over 100 miles away. We stayed in the national park for 3 days and nights, being accommodated in a very comfortable rest camp. One had to do one's own cooking. There was a very well-stocked store in the rest camp where all the necessities of life could be obtained. The Wankie National Park covers an area of 5000 square miles situated in the north west corner of Zimbabwe. All species of animals are fairly generally distributed throughout the national park, particularly elephants, buffalo, zebra, giraffe, kudu, wildebeest, roan and sable antelope, impala, waterbuck, baboon, monkeys and lion.

On 25th June we left the Wankie National Park and retraced our steps to Kariba, where a massive dam had been constructed at the north end of Lake Kariba (the largest man-made lake in the world) for the hydroelectric schemes on the Zambezi river. The area of the lake is 2000 square miles,

142

the length being 175 miles. We stayed at the Kariba Hotel on 25th and 26th June.

On 27th June we moved on to Fort Victoria and when there visited the famous Zimbabwe Ruins, first discovered by the American hunter Adam Renders in 1868. That afternoon we visited the Matopos Hills where Cecil John Rhodes, the founder of Rhodesia, was buried on 10th April 1902. The hills are of solid rock with graves hewn out of the rock. There is also a memorial to Alan Wilson and 34 men who were annihilated by the Matabele tribe on the Shangani River on 4th December 1893. On the morning of 28th June we left Zimbabwe and crossed over the border into South Africa at Beit Bridge. On the night of 28th June we were accommodated at a farmhouse at Louis Trichardt in the Transvaal. Next morning we left Louis Trichardt and drove all the way to Durban – a distance of 523 miles. We spent 4 days and nights in Durban, the largest and oldest city in the province of Natal and the biggest seaport on the east coast of Africa. The town is also a famous holiday resort, lying on the Indian Ocean with lovely sandy beaches.

After a 4-day break we set off for Cape Town, following the coast road all the way – a distance of 1000 miles. We stopped off at Umtata on 3rd July, Kidds Beach on 4th July, Seaview near Jeffreys Bay on 5th July and at Mossel Bay on 6th and 7th July. When at Mossel Bay we visited the famous Oudtshorn Ostrich Farm. On the morning of 8th July, when we were about 30 miles from Cape Town, it got much colder and we ran into sleet showers. The hills and valleys on the approach to Cape Town were very green and resembled land in England. This of course was mid-winter in the southern hemisphere.

From 8th to 12th July we stayed in a hotel in Cape Town and generally explored the area. It was our intention to visit the famous flat-topped Table Mountain but during our stay the mountain was permanently shrouded in its tablecloth of white cloud. Cape Town is the parliamentary capital and the oldest city in South Africa. It follows the curve of a natural harbour on the shoulder of the Cape peninsula and rests at the base of Table Mountain.

Deep in the heart of taxes

On the morning of 13th July we boarded the Union Castle liner *Stirling Castle* for Southampton. As the ship pulled out of the harbour that afternoon the cloud lifted and we got a lovely view of Table Mountain. The passage from Cape Town to Southampton took 14 days with a stop-over at the Canary Islands en route. We docked at Southampton on 27th July. Prior to leaving Tanganyika we had been advised by the Tanganyika government that on returning to the United Kingdom we would have to pay the British government the purchase tax on our car as by the time we got there the car would not be taxed and would have been used overseas for the stipulated time of 1 year. In view of this I had written to H. M. Customs and Excise, London, and asked them how much purchase tax I would have to pay. The reply was that the total purchase tax to be paid was £180.00 but that this could be paid in five equal instalments, the first instalment being due when the car was landed at Southampton.

By prior arrangement we were met at the Southampton docks by an AA patrolman to help us clear the car through customs. His name was Mathieson. When checking the vehicle through customs, the customs officer said that the car could not be released until the full £180.00 was paid. I explained that I had a letter from Customs House, London, stating that I only had to pay a fifth of the price to get the car released. He asked where this authority was. I said, 'Somewhere in these seven suitcases.' As I did not have £180.00 in travellers cheques, the AA patrolman asked if I had funds in a bank in the United Kingdom. I said I had a bank account with the Bank of Scotland, St Margarets Hope, Orkney. He then took me to a branch of the Midland Bank in Southampton and the problem was put to the manager there. He picked up the phone and spoke to Norman Williamson, Manager, Bank of Scotland, St Margarets Hope who confirmed that I had funds with them which would more than cover the £200.00 I requested. He then handed over £200.00. I returned to the docks with the AA patrolman after which the car was released. The patrolman then led us out of Southampton and as it was late in the afternoon he took us to small hotels and boarding houses to get accommodation for the night. The first nine claimed that they were either full up or did not cater for young children. We were accepted at the tenth attempt. The AA patrolman was marvellous and was suitably rewarded.

Private concerns

On the morning of 28th July we headed north, stopping for the night just over the Scottish border. Next day we drove on to Thurso in the north of Scotland and spent the night there before travelling over to Orkney on the *St Ola* the following day. We lived with my wife's parents for a few days at Barebreck, Widewall, South Ronaldsay and then moved to our cottage, Daisybank, near Burray village on the island of Burray, to discover to our horror that rats had moved in during our absence and had destroyed almost all the furnishings, mattresses, settee, chairs and even the padding in the pram. This was thrown out and replaced. After a month's break we decided to purchase a small general merchants' business in the village of St Margarets Hope. A large 14-roomed house went with the business, together with two stores and a garage. The price for the business and property was £1750.00. The business consisted of a mobile shop and agencies for seeds and manures. We tried to improve the business, purchasing a modern mobile shop, and reopened the shop in the village. It did not turn out to be a financial success, being unable to compete with the larger businesses in Kirkwall, and in April 1965 we closed the business down, selling the property at a later date for the sum of £1500.00.

In July 1965 we purchased a licensed grocer and cafe

business in Kincardine O'Neil, Aberdeenshire, situated between the towns of Banchory and Aboyne on Royal Deeside. The cafe did extremely well in the summer – May to September – but was dead in winter. The licensed grocer business was poor to say the least; the majority of people living in and around the village worked for lairds, many of whom lived in tied houses and were poorly paid. On 16th December 1965 our fourth child, Karen, was born at the Torphins Maternity Hospital.

During the festive season of 1965 I was selling whisky at £2.4.0 a bottle which cost £2.0.0 wholesale (the recommended retail price being £2.7.6.). Some local customers would come in and say that they could buy whisky in Aberdeen at £2.3.0. I said, 'That may be so . . .' and pointed out that it cost them 10 shillings on the bus to get there and back. During the summer months I had to employ four women to cater for the mainly passing trade going to and from Royal Deeside. As we had four young children who were inclined to be slightly neglected during the busy season we decided to give up the business. It was advertised for sale on a number of occasions and as there were no reasonable offers we again closed the business down. Before doing so I applied for a post of constable with the Admiralty Constabulary which was advertised in the *Sunday Post*.

VIII

Admiralty Constabulary and MOD Police

In October 1966 I was called to HM Naval Base, Rosyth where I was interviewed and medically examined. After being x-rayed etc., I had to go and see a civilian doctor working for the Ministry of Defence. This elderly gentleman was seated at his desk with a pile of books stacked at one corner. After asking a lot of questions he told me to get up and 'Go up and down on your haunches three times.'

While I did this he was writing away and never looked at what I was doing. On my third move up he asked if I had any injuries. I said, 'Yes – five bullet wounds.'

He shot up in his chair and said, 'What?'

I repeated what I had said. He then said that he had better have a look at them. He appeared satisfied that the wounds would not be a drawback. I was then given a sealed envelope to take to the assistant chief constable at the dockyard. When the latter opened the envelope he was surprised to find that I had failed the examination because I was half an inch too short. The official height for the Admiralty Constabulary at that time was 5 feet 7 inches or over. I was marked down at 5ft $6^{1}/_{2}$ in. I had been 5ft 7in when in the army but over the years must have lost half an inch of hair. The assistant chief constable sent a note back to the doctor asking him to change the 5ft $6^{1}/_{2}$in to 5ft 7in. This he did and I was officially accepted.

I returned to Kincardine O'Neil and arranged to auction off the entire stock, furniture, etc., in shop and cafe. A short time later I was notified by the assistant chief constable, northern area, Rosyth to report for duty at the Royal Naval Air Station, Lossiemouth on 16th November 1966. As there was no house available at the time I was accommodated in the petty officers' mess and travelled home at the weekends. I was not put on to the shift system because I had first of all to attend a 6 weeks' training course at the Admiralty Constabulary Training School at HM Dockyard, Portsmouth. On 10th January 1967 I reported to the training school as constable N 2764 on course 92. When being interviewed at the end of the course by the senior instructor who held the rank of chief inspector he said to me, 'You will never stick the force after your service in the colonial police.'

I said, 'Maybe not, but I will give it a try.'

When my post of senior superintendent of police was Africanised in 1962 I was receiving £2000.00 a year. Four years later as a constable in the Admiralty Constabulary I was receiving £680.00 per annum. On returning to Lossiemouth after the course I rented a furnished house at Rose Isle near Burghead, a short distance from the naval air station, and brought my family up from Kincardine O'Neil. A month later we were allocated a ministry of defence quarter at No. 1 Drainie Road, just outside the perimeter fence of the station at the end of the main runway. I was then on shift work – 8 hours on duty and 16 hours off. The shifts were from 6 a.m. to 2 p.m, 2 p.m. to 10 p.m. and 10 p.m. to 6 a.m. We had a regular dog man who worked from 8 a.m. to 5 p.m. days; he fed, groomed and generally looked after the dogs. At weekends a constable from the shift on duty was delegated to look after the dogs and his hours (instead of being 6 a.m. to 2 p.m.) were 8 a.m. to 4 p.m.

On one particular Saturday morning I was delegated to be dog man for the day and reported for duty at 8 a.m. After attending to the dogs I went over to the main gate and told

148

the constable on main gate duty that I would take the gate over for half an hour. At 9 a.m. every morning the duty officer of the day, a Royal Navy lieutenant accompanied by the boatswain's mate, came to the main gate to go through the daily procedure of raising the white ensign. When this occurred all traffic had to be stopped for about 3 minutes. While the ceremony was going on a car drew up at the gate; it was driven by a middle aged gentleman in civilian clothes. The ceremony over, the car drove over to the small accommodation block allocated as a rest hut for the constables on duty. As I approached the car the driver moved off slowly, did a right turn and then pulled up at the police office across the road. I approached the driver and, before I could ask him what he wanted, he said, 'Is the sub-inspector here?'

'No,' I said, 'he has been off sick for a number of months.'

He then asked, 'Is the sergeant on duty?'

I said, 'No, he works a 5-day week and is off at weekends.' I then said, 'Who are you?'

He replied, 'I am John Amos, the assistant chief constable for the northern area', and he added, 'You must be Mathieson, the new man?'

I said, 'That is correct.'

He then asked who the senior constable was and, 'Where is he now?'

I said, 'He is in the building across the road with one other constable.'

John Amos remarked, 'I did not know we owned that building,' got out of his car and headed for the rest hut.

Well, on this particular day the building was in a dreadful state. It was laid down that whenever a shift went off duty the floors had to be washed, tables washed and polished, fire tidied up and ashes disposed of. The night shift who had gone off duty at 6 a.m. that morning had not for some reason done these things. I did not know that the place was in a shambles and apart from that I had no chance to warn the constables inside of the approach of the assistant chief constable. He

149

entered the building to find the two constables slouched in seats, one with his feet on the table. The floor was in a filthy state and ashes were everywhere. We had an old-type naval stove which burnt coal for 24 hours a day. To clear the ribs one got hold of a grating under the fire bars and pulled and pushed it; this released the ashes and they dropped into the ashpan below. When doing this ashes went everywhere. On the top of the fire a large heavy-duty naval-type kettle boiled all the time and it was also in a sorry state. The assistant chief constable walked over to the fire, picked up the kettle, went straight outside and threw the kettle in the dustbin. When he came back in he told the senior constable to get an electric kettle. After giving the senior constable a severe dressing down he ordered him to go for the sergeant. I, in the meantime, was relieved at the gate by the other constable and went on patrol with one of the dogs until the dust settled.

On 18th June 1967 I was attached to the criminal investigation department H. M. Dockyard, Rosyth for 3 weeks and after returning to Lossiemouth was appointed detective constable.

Forging Links with the US Navy

On 28th October 1967 I was instructed to proceed to London to be interviewed by the chief constable of the Admiralty Constabulary, Mr F. A. Seward, concerning a post which had to be filled at Greenock. The holder of the post at the time was a sub-inspector in the CID. The post was that of liaison officer to the United States navy at the Holy Loch and the salary for the post was paid by the US navy to the Ministry of Defence. Apparently the sub-inspector had upset the commodore of the US navy at the Holy Loch as a result of which the commodore and the Royal Navy captain at Navy Buildings, Greenock, were demanding his removal. They were in fact looking for a diplomat.

I had my interview with the chief constable and was told

to report to Superintendent P. Tierney, head of the CID at Rosyth, on my way back to Lossiemouth. I duly reported to Superintendent Tierney on the afternoon of 30th October 1967 and was told that I was being transferred to Greenock the following morning to take over from the present incumbent there. I would of course be promoted to acting detective sergeant (paid) which meant a rise of over £300.00 to my annual salary. I was told to book into the Sailors' Rest in Rosyth where he, Tierney, would pick me up in the morning and take me over to Greenock.

The disappearing safe

The taking over of the post took no time. I was in, he was out. To make matters worse I was immediately faced with the theft of a safe from one of the boom defence vessels tied up at the James Watt dock, Greenock. From a check of the locus on board ship, which was the cabin allocated to the coxswain, a chief petty officer, I came to the conclusion that there was something peculiar about the break in to the cabin. The bottom of the cabin door was constructed of horizontal slats and these had been forced with a marlin spike. The drawer under the bunk, which was locked, had also been forced with the marlin spike. Valuable items in the drawer, such as an expensive camera and a Shaeffer pen, had not been taken. The safe, which was made out of quarter-inch steel plate and was bolted to the bulkhead of the ship, had completely vanished.

I was given the rough measurements of the safe. The only key to the safe was held by the coxswain, who had still not returned from weekend leave. My enquiries confirmed that the safe was mainly used for the safe keeping of funds derived from the daily ration sale of beer to the ship's crew by the boatswain, a petty officer. When collecting money due on payday the boatswain placed it in an envelope, sealed the envelope with sellotape, signed his name over the seal and recorded the amount on the outside of the envelope. He then

151

handed the envelope to the coxswain who locked it in the safe. Every second payday the boatswain handed over the two weeks' takings to the first lieutenant.

During the weekend on which the safe had gone missing the boatswain was on board ship. As it was possible to dump the safe through the porthole in the coxswain's cabin, I arranged for a diver to dive immediately below the porthole, the ship not having been moved that weekend. The diver had no difficulty in locating the safe, which was brought on board. The safe was still locked and after we had waited for an hour the coxswain returned from weekend leave. In the presence of the ship's captain and first lieutenant the coxswain opened the safe in the wardroom and handed over a sealed envelope which had the boatswain's signature and the '£70.00' written on the front of it. I opened the envelope in front of those present and found that the £70.00 which were supposed to be in the envelope were in fact pieces of paper the size of one pound notes, bound together. The boatswain was then seen and cautioned. He stated that he was in financial difficulties, knew that he would be found out on the 31st October 1967 when the accounts were to be audited and faked the break in to the coxswain's cabin, forcing the safe off the bulkhead during the weekend. Being a petty officer with over 15 years service, he was court-martialled, reduced to seaman, stripped of his three good-conduct badges and transferred to Rosyth. The sad thing about this petty officer was that his commanding officer had just recommended him for the 'Raleigh Award' for being such an able and conscientious boatswain. Two years later I ran into this man on the James Watt dock, Greenock, and was pleased to see that he had regained his rank and good-conduct badges. He invited me on board for a pint and I was delighted to accept.

After sorting out the disappearance of the safe I had to look for accommodation; for a week I stayed in a bed-and-breakfast place and then moved into the Inverclyde Sailors' Centre. In the meantime, no one had notified the Admiralty Constabulary at Lossiemouth that I had been transferred to Greenock. Man-management in those days was absolutely pathetic. I had gone to the interview with a small overnight suitcase and it was not until 6 weeks later that I got home on a visit to Lossiemouth to move house.

We were allocated No. 32 Nelson Road, Gourock – a three-bedroom MOD house. After moving in I enquired from a neighbour where the nearest primary school was. I was told it was in Binnie Street, Gourock. I drove down to Binnie Street and parked at the school. I called at reception and asked to see the headmaster. After I had given him details of the three children who were due to attend school and the name and address of their former headmaster in Burghead, the headmaster of the Binnie Street school said, 'Seeing it is Thursday afternoon there is no need for the children to come to school until Monday morning.'

As I was leaving the headmaster's study he said, 'I am sorry, I forgot to ask what your religion is?'

I said, 'I am a Presbyterian.'

He again apologised and said, 'Your school is up the street – this is a Catholic school.'

I was absolutely astounded. Heather, our eldest daughter, had gone to school with Catholics, Protestants, Muslims and Hindus, and they had all got on well together.

Although I was responsible for investigating crime in ministry of defence establishments south of the Clyde, including Greenock, Gourock, Port Glasgow, Glasgow, Beith and Stranraer, my main job was to act as the police liaison officer between the US navy and police forces throughout Scotland. My opposite number working for the United States navy was Frank Edmonds, a civilian naval intelligence officer from the United States office of naval intelligence. Frank was an ex-San Francisco police officer and was a delightful personality. He was responsible for investigating all offences which occurred on US naval establishments throughout Scotland and

Northern Ireland. I accompanied Frank on the majority of his safaris to Londonderry, Edzell, Thurso, Prestwick, Macrihanish and the Holy Loch where the drydock and mother ship to the nuclear submarines were based. We put in many long days and nights investigating all types of crimes, including one case of murder and one of attempted murder.

From 18th March 1968 until 10th May 1968 I attended an 8-week training course at the Scottish Police Detective Training School, Glasgow. Detective Constable David Barnes stood in for me during my absence. I was 42 years old at the time and had to compete with 29 detectives from all over Scotland who had been in the police force for a considerable number of years. I was therefore delighted to get the following course report at the end of training:

Scottish Police Detective Training School
Initial Detective Training Course No. 2/68

From: 18 March 1968   To: 10 May 1968

Report on: Detective Sergeant William P. Mathieson
                  Admiralty Constabulary

General Assessment
(a) *Remarks* An excellent student. Most impressive at discussion periods and the directing staff were unanimous in their opinion that Mathieson had a first class knowledge of police duties.

(b) *Examination*	*Course average*
Written 73%	71%
Oral 97.5%	89%
Date: 17th May 1968	Johnston, Det. Supt. Officer in charge

In October 1969 Detective Superintendent P. Tierney, my boss at H. M. Dockyard, Rosyth, received the following letter from Frank Edmonds.

DEPARTMENT OF THE NAVY
US NAVAL INVESTIGATIVE SERVICE OFFICE, EUROPE
FPO NEW YORK 09510

Detective Superintendent Tierney   7 October 1969
Admiralty Constabulary,
HM Dockyard, Rosyth, Fife.

Dear Superintendent Tierney,
At this time I would like to express our long overdue thanks for the outstanding manner in which detective sergeant William P Mathieson has carried out his duties as Admiralty Constabulary liaison representative with this office over the past year and one half. D. S. Mathieson has applied himself to this frequently sensitive and difficult assignment with professional efficiency, dedication and enthusiasm.

The close contact and liaison which D. S. Mathieson maintains with this office has materially aided our operations. He has done much to preserve and extend the excellent relations which exist between this office and the various law enforcement agencies and the judiciary. D. S. Mathieson is worthy of recognition for his conscientiousness, devotion to duty and cheerful willingness to work long and arduous hours in order to carry out the duties of his assignment.

Yours truly
Frank Edmonds

Occupational Hazards
Our house at 32 Nelson Road, Gourock, was one of over 100 ministry of defence houses which had been built in the first

155

world war for MOD employees who worked at the torpedo factory in Greenock. This turned out to be a problem for my wife and family. Part of my job was to investigate fraudulent claims by MOD employees for subsistence allowances and transport and official travelling claims. It was fairly common to have one or two employees trying this on, but on one occasion I had eight to deal with. Some of those were neighbours and although it did not affect me personally, the children of the employee caught took it it out on my children and this all came back to my wife, Lena, who had a lot to bear at that time.

One Saturday evening a neighbour of ours was out in his back garden under the influence of drink, cursing and swearing about the CID bastard next door. All the other neighbours were hanging out of their windows, not realising that I was away. I was in fact in Northern Ireland with Frank Edmonds and returned to Glasgow airport at 10 p.m. that night. I got home at 10.30 p.m. to find the house locked. My wife then told me what had been going on and that she and the children were terrified and had locked the doors. I went straight over to the neighbour's house to find the man and wife both almost speechless with drink. I told the woman of the house that I would see her husband in the morning when he sobered up.

At 10.30 a.m. on the Sunday morning the neighbour who had been issuing threats about the CID bastard knocked on the door. I opened the door and he started to apologise. I said, 'There is no use in apologising to me; go into the house and apologise to my wife, and furthermore you are to be reported to the Resident Naval Officer, Navy Buildings, Greenock, about your conduct.'

He did go in, very sheeplishly, and apologised to my wife. On the next day, Monday, I related the facts to the said resident naval officer. My neighbour was called in front of the RNO and was warned that if there was a repetition of such conduct he and his family would be immediately evicted from the MOD house. This had a salutary effect.

Returning to my work with the US navy, at the outset, when I boarded the *USS Canopus*, mother ship to the nuclear submarines in the Holy Loch, I was classed as a foreigner and my movements on board ship were very restricted. If I was accompanied by Frank Edmonds, Frank was held responsible for me but I nevertheless had to wear a large badge bearing the word 'Uncleared'. If I was called on board ship on my own, I was met on the quarter deck by an armed marine who escorted me to the place of visit, stayed with me and escorted me off the ship when my business was over. I also had to wear the badge.

Down to cases

After a year or so I was allowed to come and go at will, only having to check in and out on the quarter deck of the ship. One or two cases of interest which Frank and I dealt with are appended below.

The first case was a tip-off that divers from the *USS Simon Lake*, replacement for the *USS Canopus*, when going on practice diving in Loch Long, were landing goods near the village of Blairmore about halfway up the loch. We arranged with the executive officer of the ship to notify us when the next diving practice was to take place. About 2 weeks later we got a call one evening that the diving boat was going out at 8 a.m. on the following morning. Frank and I travelled over on the early Gourock/Dunoon ferry and positioned ourselves on the east side of the Holy Loch across from the *USS Simon Lake* and kept a watch on the ship. At 8 a.m. we saw the diving boat leaving the *Simon Lake* and headed out of the loch. As the road followed the side of the loch we kept the diving boat in sight without any difficulty; when clearing the mouth of the Holy Loch it turned into the entrance to Loch Long. Again, there was no difficulty in following the progress of the boat. We drove on past Blairmore village, hid the car up a wooded track and moved into a forest reserve with binoculars.

The diving boat stopped just beyond Blairmore village.

The crew then launched a rubber dinghy and we could see them loading items into the dinghy. A few minutes later two of the crew boarded the rubber dinghy, started up the outboard and headed for the shore. As we were only 200 yards away we continued to watch and at that moment a white Volkswagen car, coming from the direction of Ardentinney, stopped as the rubber dinghy was approaching the beach. On beaching the craft, the driver of the car went down on the beach to meet the two crew members and the three of them carried items up the beach which were placed at the side of the Volkswagen. We came out of hiding at that point and removed the ignition key from the Volkswagen. We found that items landed included a freezer box, tarpaulins, diving lights, hammers, saws, etc. The driver of the Volkswagen turned out to be a US navy petty officer, also a diver, who lived in the area and was off duty.

The crew members of the rubber dinghy were also divers with the rank of petty officer. Their service details were recorded and they were ordered to return to the *USS Simon Lake*. The ship was contacted and notified what had been going on and was asked to obtain the names of the divers who had remained on board the diving boat. Frank and I seized all the stolen goods and after the petty officers had been court-martialled the stolen goods were returned to the ship. They were alleged to be presents for the local farmers in the area.

Another incident concerning the *USS Simon Lake* was when the ship's special services office was broken into and 850 dollars stolen from a home-made safe which had been forced. A padlock secured the door to the special services office. One side of the padlock hasp had been cut with bolt croppers, and after the job of entering and forcing the safe door and stealing the contents of the safe had been done, the padlock hasp had been swung back into position. So although the door to the office was checked on a number of occasions during the night and early morning by night security staff the break in to the office was only discovered at 7 a.m. in the morning when the office staff went to work. The safe was constructed of quarter-inch steel and was bolted to a steel partition of the office, about 5 feet from the deck. The offender had managed to get the point of a heavy-duty screwdriver into the top right-hand corner of the safe (the hinged side of the safe), and force the corner down a short distance. He had then climbed up pipes running along the wall of the office (leaving fingerprints on pipes), and with his feet had bent the top right-hand corner of the safe door down sufficiently to enable him to get his hand in through the gap he'd made. The money in the safe was contained in a cash box, he managed to turn this over and retrieve the cash – 850 dollars. Cheques in the cash box were left behind.

On examining the safe door for fingerprints I came up with two beautiful prints which turned out to be a forefinger and middle finger of a right hand. The prints were located behind the mechanism of the lock on the inside of the door and the angle and position of the prints were such that they could only be those of the offender. It was decided to fingerprint everyone on board – a total of 1200 men. Priority was given to fingerprinting those going on leave, transfer or leaving the service. I commenced this task on board ship in an office behind the store commander's office. I fingerprinted 50 a day and dispatched the prints the same evening to HM Dockyard, Rosyth, where Detective Sergeant Jones checked them out.

On the morning of the 6th day, 250 sets of prints having been sent to Rosyth, I received a call from the detective sergeant stating that we had got him. This was a Thursday morning. The offender was a coloured seaman. I relayed the information to Frank Edmonds who passed on the information to the executive officer of the USS *Simon Lake*, with the request that the offender be sent over to Greenock under escort to be interviewed and charged. The executive officer rang back to say that the wanted man had been granted local leave to get married in Glasgow on Saturday. The executive officer had no idea where the marriage was to take place and knew only that he was due to return to the ship in 2 weeks' time. Frank passed this information on to me; our only way of finding out when and where the marriage was to take place would be to contact the registrars of births, marriages and deaths in Glasgow. After checking the telephone directory I found there were six such offices in Glasgow. I rang them all and although all were extremely courteous and helpful none of the offices had any record of the offender getting married on the Saturday in question.

In the circumstances all we could do was to wait until the seaman returned from his local leave. However, as I was about to lock up my office and go home I got a call from one of the registrars stating that the offender had just been in with a special licence from the sheriff's office enabling him to get married on Saturday. I was given his local address in Glasgow as well as the address of the woman he was marrying. At 7 a.m. on the Friday morning Frank and I called at the offender's address in Glasgow but got no reply to repeated knocks on the door. His address was a flat in a tenement block. When descending the communal stairs we spoke to a Pakistani woman who lived in one of the flats and asked if she knew this sailor. She said she did, that he was getting married on Saturday and that she was sure he was living with his future in-laws.

We dashed off to this address and knocked on the door. The door was opened by a middle-aged Glaswegian male. After identifying ourselves we asked if the offender was in the house. He said he was and that he was still in bed. We then explained what the problem was. He said, 'Come in, go upstairs and you'll find him in the bedroom.'

This we did; he was cautioned, charged and arrested. He was due to marry a nurse from Glasgow the following morning. He was court-martialled on board *USS Simon Lake* and was sentenced to 6 months' detention. On his release the marriage went ahead.

When visiting the US Navy Base, Edzell, Forfar, in 1971 we were advised by the executive officer there, a US navy commander, that he was not entirely happy with the duty-free situation on the station. As a privilege, HM Customs and Excise granted certain duty-free privileges to US servicemen in this country and with regard to spirits this was that married couples could purchase six 40 oz bottles of spirits a month and single men four 40 oz bottles. The executive officer stated that when checking the duty-free chits – the chits or ration coupons that the buyer handed over before getting his duty-free allocation – he was astounded to find that a young seaman who was definitely a non-drinker and a great churchgoer and a superintendent of the Sunday School had been purchasing his full ration of four 40 oz bottles of spirits for over a year. The navy commander had been so surprised by this that he'd called in this young seaman and asked what was going on. The seaman quite openly said that he had been asked by a petty officer to purchase his ration of spirits and that he, the petty officer, would buy it off him as he sometimes ran short of drink at parties.

Frank and I had a word with this young sailor and he mentioned that the petty officer he was supplying with drink was also buying drink from other sailors who did not require their full quota. It was then decided to have a word with the petty officer. It turned out that the petty officer was a keen amateur racing driver and took part in competitions at the Ingliston Racing Circuit, Edinburgh. During interview he stated that he had been bartering 40 oz bottles of spirits for spare parts for his sports car, particularly the very expensive racing tyres. He supplied the name of a garage in Forfar which he dealt with. Further information about other deals came to light during these enquiries, the most interesting one being a deal between a sailor on the base and the manager of a hotel in Edzell. The deal was that the manager would sell a 1953 Rover car, valued at £350.00, to the sailor for six cases of 40 oz bottles of vodka – 72 bottles in all. This was a lucrative deal all round. A 40 oz bottle of vodka in the United Kingdom at the time cost £5.00 and with 72 bottles at £5.00 a piece the manager was getting £360.00 in value for his car which he could double by selling the spirit over the bar. The sailor on the other hand also had a good deal. He was only paying 15 shillings for a 40 oz bottle of duty-free vodka, the total cost of 72 bottles coming to £54.00. By the time we caught up with and interviewed the sailor, 29 bottles had changed hands.

As these were customs offences Frank and I called on the Customs Investigation Branch in Glasgow and related the facts to them. Mr Cadogan of the CIB was asked to investigate the cases with us. As Frank was called away on other urgent business I was asked to accompany Mr Cadogan to Edzell, Forfar and Brechin to investigate the various reported offences. Our first port of call was the Glen Esk Hotel, Edzell. As we walked into the lounge bar we noted straight away two duty-free 40 oz bottles of vodka behind the bar. The manager was called, cautioned and questioned about his possession of duty-free spirits. The customs officer produced the Customs Writ (search warrant), seized the two partly full bottles from behind the bar and asked to be taken to the liquor store in the hotel. In the cellar of the hotel five full 40 oz bottles of duty-free vodka were seized. The manager was then charged and when he appeared in the Sheriff court, Forfar, at a later date he was found guilty and fined £75.00.

During these investigations the names of a number of farmers in the area were mentioned, and as one was mentioned on more than one occasion a visit was made to his farm. The farmer and his wife who were in their mid-sixties, looked very worried when Cadogan explained the reason for his visit to the farmhouse. When asked if he had any duty-free goods in the house, the farmer said that he had a few packets of duty-free cigarettes in his bedroom upstairs. The farmer, Cadogan and I made our way upstairs and after a short delay the farmer found the key to his locked bedside cabinet, opened it up and produced a carton of Winston cigarettes containing eight packets of 20 cigarettes. In the bedroom there was also a part case of Budweizer beer. We then went back downstairs to the living room and Cadogan went across to the drinks cabinet in the corner of the room and opened the doors. All it contained were British spirits. I noticed that before Cadogan had opened up the cabinet the farmer had been looking very worried, but now he was completely relaxed. I thought this rather strange.

Cadogan thanked them for their cooperation and we left. As I was going out through the porch I lifted the lid off a bin which revealed bottles of spirits, cigarettes, tinned food, etc. These were seized by Cadogan and the farmer was charged. It just went to show that you cannot leave a suspect alone when investigating a crime. The farmer's elderly wife had all her faculties about her. As soon as we headed up to the bedroom she collected all the duty-free goods and dumped them in the bin. The change in the facial expressions of both the farmer and his wife was a dead give away but finding where she'd put them was a stroke of luck.

When we left the house we ran into a warrant officer from the base at Edzell who had just arrived at the farm to barter a 40 oz bottle of whisky for a sack of potatoes. He also lost his bottle and was dealt with by the US naval authorities. As the elderly farmer suffered a slight heart attack after the visit by the customs officer, his doctor notified the prosecutor fiscal and the case against him was dropped. A lot of bartering that went on for potatoes and poultry was good public relations and would never have come to light had someone not got too greedy and spoilt it for the genuine people who were not making a racket out of it.

Examinations and conferences

Although I was appointed an acting detective sergeant on 1st November 1967 with less than a year's service in the force, I still had to sit and pass the constable to sergeants' examination before being considered for promotion to the rank of sergeant. I therefore sat and passed the examination on 7th January 1970 and was subsequently promoted to the rank of sergeant on 7th May 1970. On 1st October 1971 the Admiralty Constabulary, air force departmental constabulary and the army departmental constabulary were all amalgamated into the MOD police force.

On 9th January 1973 Mr Frank Edmonds, Special Agent, US Naval Investigative Service office, Greenock, sent the following letter to the Detective Superintendent, Ministry of Defence Police, HM Dockyard, Rosyth:

Dear Sir,
I would like to take this opportunity to express the gratitude of the US Naval Investigative Services Office, Europe, and my own personal appreciation for the continued outstanding support which Detective Sergeant Mathieson has provided to this office over the past 5 years.

Detective Sergeant Mathieson has worked closely with this office on numerous important and sensitive investigations over the years and his assistance and expertise have contributed in large measure to the successful resolution of a high proportion of those investigations. He has been diligent in maintaining a close and harmonious working relationship with police authorities throughout Scotland which has materially aided our operations.

His readiness to assist us at any time of the day or night, often at great inconvenience to himself and family, and his concern to give us a fair share of his busy schedule have been greatly appreciated. Detective Sergeant Mathieson is an outstanding police officer and a credit to your organisation.
Yours truly
F. J. Edmonds
Special Agent

On 15th February 1973 I sat and passed the promotion

examination from sergeant to higher rank and was promoted to the rank of sub-inspector on the 1st May 1974 following which I was transferred to the Central Ordnance Depot, Chilwell, near Beeston, Nottinghamshire. Before departing for Chilwell I was called to Edzell where I was presented with the base plaque and a letter of appreciation from the Commanding Officer, Captain W. K. Martin. The letter reads as follows:

25.4.74

Detective Sergeant William P. Mathieson,
Ministry of Defence Police,
Greenock, Scotland.

It is with great pleasure upon the occasion of your transfer to Ministry of Defence Police, Nottingham, England that I commend you for the sustained outstanding liaison, assistance and support you have provided this command for the past five years.

As liaison officer assigned to the US Naval Investigative Service, your professional competence and skills have proven invaluable to the successful mission accomplishment of this command. Your willingness to work long and tedious hours in fulfilling your responsibilities, coupled with your expertise, has resulted in the fruitful completion of all your investigative endeavours.

The fairness and impartiality which you have brought to bear in the conduct of criminal investigations represents the highest possible standard of law enforcement, and evidences your sincere concern for the administration of justice. Equally commendable has been the excellent rapport you established and maintained with Scottish law enforcement and judicial authorities in the area. Your efforts in fostering harmonious and cooperative working relationships with these authorities have contributed significantly towards the preservation and enhancement of the reputation of this command.

You can indeed be proud of your achievements and contributions of the past 5 years. The outstanding professional assistance you have provided this command reflects very highly upon yourself and the Ministry of Defence Police. It is indeed a pleasure to extend my personal 'Well done' for the outstanding service you provided to this command and to congratulate you on your upcoming promotion. Additionally I would like to extend my best wishes to you and your family for continued success and happiness in the future.

W. K. Martin
Captain US Navy
Commanding Officer

My duties at the Central Ordnance Depot, Chilwell were to investigate and supervise the investigation into crimes which occurred at that depot and at all other ministry of defence establishments from Nottinghamshire to the Scottish border east of the Pennine chain. My staff at Chilwell comprised Detective Sergeant Ian Ford, Detective Constables Mike Hughes and Geoff Avison and, generally, one or two constables being trained for the CID.

The crimes which we had to deal with were usually run of the mill offences: thefts, fraud, burglaries, etc. We had one serious case of arson in May 1975 which took place at the Central Ordnance Depot, Chilwell, as I was about to depart on a 10-week Metropolitan Police senior detective course at the Hendon Police College, London. It turned out that the fire, which cost around £1 000 000 in damage, was caused by a storehouseman deliberately setting fire to wood wool in crates and then attempting to put the fire out himself. He had fallen out with his girl friend and this was his attempt to win her back. He was, however, unable to contain the blaze which completely destroyed a massive warehouse and its contents. For this he was sentenced to 3 years' imprisonment.

Two months after taking over the MOD police CID office at Chilwell, I attended, along with Detective Sergeant Ford and Detective Constable Hughes, a 3-day CID conference of the Central area at Chorley in Lancashire. Accommodation was booked for us by a detective sergeant from the Central area, CID headquarters, Cheadle Hulme. When shown the accommodation, which was one fairly large room with three single beds, one wardrobe, one chest of drawers and a thread-bare square of carpeting (and no wash basin), we walked out. In and around the Chorley area we tried for accommodation at three establishments but all were full up.

As Chorley was near the Preston Police Training School, Detective Constable Hughes, who had attended a 10-week course at the school, mentioned that he had been told, when there, that if ever he was in the area and could not get accommodation he should come to the school to see if they could assist. We decided to give it a try. On arriving at the administration block, my two colleagues went in and spoke to the duty sergeant. He was not sure if we could be accommodated and asked to see their warrant cards. Detective Sergeant Ford was then asked to call me in.

People entering the foyer were able to see photographs of all the instructing staff. When glancing at the photographs I was amazed to find that the photograph at the top of the display, depicting the commandant of the college, was of Arthur Filbey; he had served in Tanganyika on secondment from the Lancashire Constabulary as an assistant commissioner of police. Arthur was well known to me and when I approached the duty sergeant and told him that I was well known to the commandant he turned to my two officers and told them they could throw their warrant cards away. The duty sergeant said that the commandant was still in his office – it was now 6.30 p.m. – and added that his wife was due to open a flower show in the college at 7 p.m. The sergeant pointed out the commandant's office to me. I went over, knocked on the door and walked in. Arthur was delighted to see me and from his cocktail cabinet produced a dram for both of us. We were immediately supplied with individual rooms in the college for the duration of the conference. Nice to have friends in important positions.

On the 2nd September 1974 the post of sub-inspector was abolished in the MOD police and with effect from that date I was appointed a detective inspector.

IX

Flotta Terminal

As I was not particularly taken up with the English criminal law and all the paper work involved in recording voluntary statements, caution statements, etc. (completely foreign to the simpler and to my mind more effective Scottish system), I was looking for a change in employment and applied to Occidental of Britain Inc., who were starting to recruit personnel for their terminal on the island of Flotta in the Orkney Islands. On 7th October 1975 I was interviewed in London for a post in the security division. Following the interview I was advised that they were only recruiting security guards at the time and that they did not have a suitable post to offer me. On 1st March 1976 I received a telegram from the training and safety superintendent, Occidental, Flotta, asking that I telephone Hoy 301. When I did so I was told that I was being offered the post of security supervisor at Flotta subject to an interview with the deputy terminal manager, Captain A. R. MacKay, set for 10 a.m. on 17th March 1976. Occidental made arrangements for the flight from Castle Donnington to Kirkwall on 16th March and the return flight two days later.

At 10 a.m. on the morning of 17th March I called at Craigiefield House, Kirkwall, to see Captain MacKay. His secretary was about to take me to his office when he emerged with the terminal manager. The secretary introduced me,

169

upon which Captain MacKay said, 'We are in a hurry to go to the airport to meet some United States company officials. I know all about you; if you want the job it's yours, I will see you in the Torvaug bar at lunchtime for a beer. In the meantime go to the Kirkwall Hotel where we have offices rented, get your photograph taken and listen in to orientation lectures which are going on there.'

At midday I had a beer with Captain MacKay and after lunch was given a conducted tour of the Flotta terminal by Bill Read, the deputy fire and safety officer. We returned to Kirkwall in the evening and reported to Captain MacKay. Captain MacKay then said, 'You and your wife's parents are in South Ronaldsay aren't they?'

I said, 'Indeed they are.'

He turned to Bill Read and said, 'Get him a car so that he can visit his parents and in-laws and he can leave the car at the airport in the morning before he returns to Nottingham.'

It was agreed that I would start with the company on 1st June 1976. I had never in my life had such star treatment from an employer.

We returned to Orkney on 25th May 1976 and moved in with my wife's parents at Barebreck, Widewall, South Ronaldsay. Heather, our eldest daughter, remained in Beeston, Nottinghamshire, where she was employed as a dispenser with Boots the chemist.

Establishing security

I reported for work at the Flotta terminal on 1st June and found that my security staff numbered five guards. As the terminal was still in the early days of construction it was impossible to enforce any definite form of security. As I was left to organise the security from scratch, with no supervision or guidance, I based the terminal security on similar lines to those adopted at MOD establishments. First of all, to get a record of all those who were working on the terminal, I photographed all Occidental employees; everyone was issued with a photographic identity card. I then concentrated on the 1200 construction workers who lived on site together with another 100 or so who travelled to and from work daily. With regard to the contractors' employees, all I was supplied with was a company nominal roll which gave no details of each individual's home address, next of kin, etc. Backgrounds to the photographs were of different colours to differentiate between those accommodated on site, those entitled to a midday meal and those not entitled to meals.

Prior to the introduction of the identity card system all visitors to Flotta, whether connected with work on the terminal or not, walked freely into the dining halls and availed themselves of very good meals. Towards the end of 1976 security had to be tightened, mainly from the safety point of view as oil was due to flow into the terminal before the end of the year. This meant seeing that temporary fences and road blocks were erected where the permanent security fence had not yet been established owing to ongoing construction work.

Oil started flowing into the terminal on 26th December 1976. There was a rule whereby all Occidental staff and contractors' employees had to surrender all matches, lighters, battery operated radios, etc., to security at the main gate to the operational area of the terminal. Contractors' employees proceeding to work would, on occasions, however, deliberately take matches, lighters and transistor radios with them into the terminal. Those caught with matches and lighters in their possession were immediately dismissed and sent off the island. After about nine employees had been caught and dismissed the message got home.

The first tanker was loaded with crude oil on the 11th January 1977 at the official opening of the terminal by Dr Armand Hammer, chairman and chief executive of the Occidental Petroleum Corporation and the Right Honourable Tony Benn, secretary of state for energy. In early December 1976 we moved to Occidental rented accommodation at Stenness on the mainland of Orkney and remained there until

171

11th February 1977 when we moved to Flotta. Mr John Hogg, who had been terminal manager from the beginning, moved to Aberdeen in June 1977 and was replaced by Gary Lavis in the same month. On 1st July 1977 my staff was increased from five to twelve.

Matters for the council

With local elections coming up in May 1978 I was approached by locals who asked me to stand for the Flotta community council. I said that as I had only been on the island for a year it would be wrong for me to stand as a councillor. This was not, however, accepted. On the Sunday evening prior to the close of nominations for the council, which had to arrive at the council offices, Kirkwall, by 5 p.m. on the next day, Monday, I had a visit from two local Flottarians, namely Tom Sutherland and Jimmy Stanger. Each was in possession of a half bottle of whisky; they also had a nomination form filled out – all it lacked was my signature. After a few drams and a lot of arm twisting I finally relented and signed the form.

At the first meeting of the Flotta community council (late May 1978) I was elected chairman; and I did not get out of the chair until the elections, 4 years later. At about the same time (end of April 1978) a convention was held in the Flotta school to discuss the long-term implications of the terminal in Flotta and how this would affect the community. Discussions were also held to formulate proposals/plans for future community activities in the new community centre which was under construction at that time. A sore point at that period was that the island of Flotta was being served by a doctor who was an assistant to the doctor stationed in the neighbouring island of Hoy. As a result of this, for 2 years, the locals had had to put up with locums, some of whom stayed for very short periods; this had an unsettling effect on the islanders, the majority of whom were elderly. However, in February 1978 Dr Iain McNicol and his family arrived in Flotta, again as an assistant to the doctor in Hoy but on a year's contract. As there was not much future for Iain and his family – not having his own general practice – the Flotta community council took this up and badgered the local member of parliament, Orkney Health Board and the Secretary of State for Scotland. It was pointed out that it was essential to have a career-orientated doctor in Flotta with his own practice to look after the local population of 180 people, 1200 contractors on site and other workers (100–150) who travelled to and from Flotta daily.

We were very fortunate in that Occidental's public relations officer, Bill Crichton, attended the majority of the community council meetings as an observer and naturally kept Occidental's terminal manager, Gary Lavis, up to date with the local problems. After battling with the Health Board and the Secretary of State for about a year, Occidental solved the problem by offering to pay £10 000 a year for 10 years to the Health Board as part of the cost of Flotta having its own doctor. This was accepted and Dr Iain McNicol got his own practice.

The new community centre was completed in early 1979 and was officially opened on 23rd February 1979. The building cost £240 000. The Flotta residents' share of one quarter of the cost was paid by Occidental. To go along with the new community centre, and as it was the international Year of the Child, the Flotta community council then embarked on organising a playing field for the children. Three acres of land above the Burnside housing estate which belonged to the education department of the Orkney Islands Council was obtained for this purpose.

I had heard at the time that F. M. C. Lilley Ltd., contractors on the terminal, had received a consignment of galvanised chain link fencing which did not comply with the height and standard required for the terminal owing to an error by their quantity surveyor on site. The fencing was in fact 4 feet high instead of 6 feet – fencing used at the time as temporary security fencing. As it would cost a lot of money to return the consignment south and as it was doubtful that the supplier would accept it back it lay out in all weathers in a lay down area of the terminal. I had a word with Jim MacDonald, site manager, F. M. C. Lilley Ltd., and told him about our project. He immediately offered to supply sufficient fencing to fence in the 3 acres of land at no cost.

Strainers for the fence in the form of railway sleepers, plus sufficient concrete to set them in, was given by Ernie Gilroy and Lou Anderson, director and site agent respectively of Hewden contracts. Local residents Ernie Cooper and his son Richard ploughed the field, Danny Barnett rotated it and Willie Robertson harrowed it. As the ground still required a certain amount of levelling Bill Davenport, Sandy Cameron, John Eadie and George Whyte of Hewden Landscaping came up after work with a massive tractor. With five railway sleepers towed behind it, the tractor soon levelled the ground. The only cost to the community council of the playing field project was the purchase of grass seed, and wages to Kenny Laird to erect the fence.

To show the appreciation of the Flotta community council for the help given and materials supplied free of charge a dance was held in the community centre on 19th October 1979 when scrolls and inscribed medals were presented to all the contractors and locals who helped with the playing field. On 1st October 1979 four more security guards were recruited, making the security staff 16 strong. At the same time we moved into the new security building directly above Gibraltar Pier and took over all the construction area which hitherto had been the responsibility of contract security employed by the Occidental Engineering Company. The 16 security personnel were divided into four shifts of four men with a lead security guard (sergeant) in charge of each shift. With leave, sickness, etc., this ensured that there were a minimum of three men on each shift. Contract security personnel still manned the airport.

In mid-December 1979, apart from a skeleton staff, all contractors' employees went on leave for the Christmas and

New Year holidays. I then took the opportunity to tighten up security appreciably by introducing a registration card, containing all relevant personal particulars, for every employee. Everyone was issued with a new photographic identity card on his/her return from leave.

Critical decision

As is normal in any large ongoing construction a certain amount of pilfering occurs. However, the scale of pilfering on Flotta was insignificant because (Flotta being an island) all contractors and terminal staff had to travel by launch. Anything they carried with them which looked unusual or heavy was quickly spotted. In this connection two of my security guards shared a vehicle with an electrician who was an Occidental employee.

On one particular weekend they were on night shift from Friday to Sunday, 7 p.m. to 7 a.m. On the Saturday morning when going off shift the electrician, who was also a shop steward, was carrying a black plastic bag containing something quite heavy. The guards had no chance to check the bag and had no reasonable reason for doing so. On the Sunday morning when going off shift the electrician was carrying another black plastic bag containing a heavy item. On arriving at Houton the electrician put the black plastic bag in his car and said that he had to make a phone call from the waiting room. When he was away the guards checked the bag and found part of an electric motor.

I was not informed of the guards' suspicions until they returned to work on day shift the following Wednesday. After they had related the facts to me I went to see the electrical supervisor, only to find that he was off sick. When he returned on Friday I gave him the details. He said that they had 12 such motors on site and that he would physically check them all. On the afternoon of Friday he rang to say that all motors had been accounted for.

On the following Monday morning the electrical super-

175

visor called at my office and reported that an electric motor was missing. It was a non-intrinsically safe electric motor (could not be used on the terminal) which had been sent by a company in the south of England. He contacted the company when he discovered that it could not be used in the terminal and said that he would return it to them. The company requested that the motor be retained in Flotta until they had other electrical items to return for servicing. The motor was placed on a shelf in the electrical storeroom and was no longer there.

Normally in such circumstances I would have gone to the terminal manager to appraise him of the facts and get approval to go ahead and notify the police of my suspicions. However, knowing that the terminal manager and deputy terminal manager had that weekend just returned from attending a difficult tribunal hearing in Aberdeen, I was sure that the terminal manager would not have let me proceed with the investigation, especially in view of the fact that the suspect was a shop steward. Knowing that my head might roll if things went wrong I took it upon myself to find out all the facts. I contacted the detective sergeant, Kirkwall police station, and related the information to him, giving such details as the make of the electric motor, serial number, etc. The detective sergeant considered that there was sufficient evidence to obtain a search warrant; he obtained the warrant and searched a house in South Ronaldsay where he recovered the electric motor and other suspect items.

The accused was arrested and locked up on the Monday night; he appeared in court on Tuesday, pled guilty to the theft of the electric motor and was fined £50.00. Another item seized was a bridge megger valued at £500.00. This item was purchased by Occidental in 1974, during the early days of construction, and loaned to the contracting company, Turiff Taylor Tarmac; it had never been returned. The accused was formerly an employee of Turiff Taylor Tarmac. He was charged with the theft of the bridge megger, fined heavily and subsequently dismissed.

On the arrest of the shop steward on the Monday afternoon I notified the terminal manager of what had been going on and put it to him that had I asked his permission to go ahead with the enquiry he would not have allowed me to do so. He said that as the individual was a shop steward and because of the lapse of time (a week) during which the motor could have been disposed of, he would not have sanctioned the action which I had undertaken. He was, however, delighted with the outcome.

Pre-retirement memories

By mid-1980 a large part of the construction work had been completed and by mid-August 1980 the construction staff on site consisted of 21 staff members and 158 workers. They were in general finishing off jobs and landscaping the terminal.

On 30th January 1981 Dr Iain McNicol, the Flotta doctor, following the sudden illness of his father, also a doctor, left Flotta to take over his father's practice at Port Appin, Argyllshire. Prior to leaving Flotta, Iain and his wife, Winnie, attended a farewell function in the community centre at which they were presented with the following gifts: from the Flotta community council and Flotta residents, a pendulum clock and silver salver, both suitably engraved, and six Edinburgh crystal glasses; from the Flotta construction social club, a crystal decanter and six crystal glasses; from Grand Metropolitan caterers, a silver salver; and from Balfour Kilpatrick and F. M. C. Lilley Ltd., a crystal fruit bowl. The terminal management had already laid on a buffet lunch for Iain and his wife (21 January) and had presented them with a crystal decanter and a bottle of 12-year-old Highland Park Whisky. When it is considered that Iain and his wife had only been on the island for 3 years their popularity was incredible, as evidenced by the gifts showered on them.

Iain was replaced by a locum for the months of February

177

and March 1981. A day or two after arriving on Flotta the doctor visited the construction social club where he was right royally entertained. After he had been in the club a couple of hours one of my guards received a telephone call from the doctor's wife asking if security had seen her husband. She was advised that her husband was in the club and that they would notify her when he left. The social club was just below the security building and outside the terminal. About half an hour later the doctor headed home but did not make it. He ended up in the ditch on the wrong side of the road. His progress up the hill was watched by security and there came a time when the car was not moving but its headlights remained on.

Raymond Stanger and Norrie Firth, two of my biggest guards, went to investigate and found the doctor very drunk with his car well and truly ditched. They pulled the car out of the ditch with their Land-Rover and delivered the doctor and his car to his house at Springbank, Flotta. The doctor's wife, a very pleasant lady, was very upset when the two guards more or less carried the doctor up the front steps. She thought the guards were policemen (blue uniforms) and was very relieved to find out that they were not. Rumours were rife about the doctor drinking and on one occasion I was asked by another doctor to keep an eye on him and report on his drinking. I said that I had no intention of doing so and if they wanted to catch him they would have to do their own sleuthing. However, towards the end of March 1981 two of my guards, on returning from lunch, reported that the doctor was in the foyer of the Occidental Residential Building and appeared to be under the influence of drink because as they were passing he came to attention and called out, 'Here comes the Gestapo.'

I went down for lunch to find the doctor leaning over the counter of the shop annoying the shop assistant. Under his arm he had a bundle of confidential files belonging to patients. I advised him to go home immediately with his files, and that if he would not do so I would take more serious action. He refused to go. I contacted the male nursing staff

178

and told them to ring the medical officer of health (MOH), health board, Kirkwall and report on the state of their doctor. This was done and the same afternoon the MOH came over to Flotta and took the doctor away. On 1st April 1981 a permanent general practitioner was posted to Flotta.

On 31st July 1981 construction work finally ended and the remaining construction security guards were paid off, with the exception of Jim Simpson who was in charge of the Flotta airstrip which now came under my umbrella. Jim, a former regular soldier in the Gordon Highlanders, ex-prisoner of war in Poland and ex fire chief for Caithness, Sutherland, Orkney and Shetland, was an outstanding man. He was one of the old school who called a spade a spade. He trained all 16 lead security guards and security guards in fire training at the airstrip to standards expected by the civil aviation authority. The guards were turned out and tested at least once a year by an official from that authority. When aircraft landed or took off a team of three (the airstrip chief and two security guards) had to be present at all times. They also had to carry out the documentation of all passengers arriving and departing. One of the three manned the ground-to-air radio, giving wind speeds and directions etc., and the other two were in the fire appliance with engine running ready to proceed to any emergency on the airstrip.

On 20th April 1983 a twin otter coming in to land at the Flotta airstrip at a time when there was a very strong crosswind, caught the runway with the tip of the starboard wing; the aircraft was flipped on its back and came to rest at the side of the runway. There were 11 passengers on board. One or two passengers received cuts and bruises but there were no serious injuries. Jim Simpson, the airstrip chief, and his two assistants, security guards Maurice Baikie and Gordon Sandison, were on the scene of the crash within one minute and put out a smouldering fire in the port engine. All passengers were evacuated within 3 minutes.

On 31st December 1984 Jim Simpson retired and returned to his home in Thurso. On Jim's departure the arrival and departure of aircraft at Flotta came under the control of the duty lead security guard. By this time flights into Flotta were greatly reduced.

By mid–1985 as the post of security supervisor became a very routine affair and as I always intended to retire on my 60th birthday, I put in a request to retire on 30th June 1985; this was accepted. During my 9 years and 1 month as security supervisor I served under four terminal managers all of whom gave me their wholehearted support. Not one of them questioned or queried any part of the security set up on the terminal. For this I thank them.